THE INTERNATIONAL ADVANTAGE

THE INTERNATIONAL ADVANTAGE

GET NOTICED. GET HIRED!

MARCELO BARROS

Barros Books

Published by Barros Books

Library of Congress Control Number: 2015908819

ISBN 978-0-692-46315-4

Typesetting services by BOOKOW.COM

CONTENTS

PROLOGUE

A quick Google search for "jobs in the U.S. and international students" turns up articles that indicate international students are practically forced to leave the United States after graduation. Many of these articles do not cite legitimate data sources and contain half-baked information, making it hard for readers to correctly interpret exactly what is going on. Drama sells. Add "H-1B," and "international students" to a headline and your article may go viral.

When I analyze international students and their desire to work in the United States after graduation, I remind myself to take a deep breath and approach the subject with logic, a balanced perspective, and reliable data. The fact is, since its inspection in 1990, no major changes have been made to the H-1B visa program, the visa that most international students must secure in order to work in the United States after graduation.

After President Trump was elected, many people incorrectly identified changes in the H-1B program that were never actually made, overreacting to bills that never became laws and devising job-search strategies based on rumors or, in some instances, false information. Sadly, many international students believed that tougher employment conditions required new job-search strategies, including, perhaps, serious reconsideration of whether they should seek jobs in a country other than the United States.

Let me tell you something: the American Dream may be hard to attain but it has always been alive. International student job search success is more than possible.

Positive New Trends

While many international students continue to find success in the technology sector because a lack of qualified American workers leaves many tech jobs unfilled, highly skilled international students who are true value creators can also find jobs in engineering, healthcare, education, business, and several other sectors. For example, *The International Advantage* has seen great international student job-search success coming from Texas A&M University School of Public Health, a school we have worked with since 2015. The bottom line is this: it is not only international computer science majors who get hired.

One could say that it comes down to being a superior job seeker and having more muscle power than your competition. Of course, as described in Chapter 3: "It's Great to Be an International STEM Major," some fields are more international student-friendly than others. Regardless of what you choose to study, you will not get hired as an international student who needs a visa by being average. A question that internationals who seek U.S. employment must always ask is this: Am I in the top 10% of job applicants who want this role? *The International Advantage* wants to help you be part of the 10%!

Some Succeed. Some Don't.

MBA Luiz Henrique De Geroni secured a great position as Director of Finance at L'Oréal in New York City after graduation, but L'Oréal was forced to relocate Luiz to Canada when he received bad news from the

H-1B lottery. Large companies like L'Oréal, which have offices around the world, might be able to transfer an international hire who did not get lucky with the lottery to another country and then try the H-1B lottery again another year, for example.

Similarly, Aditya Padman, one of the strongest investment banking career-transitioning MBAs I have worked with, secured two quality job offers after graduation, only to also receive bad news from the H-1B lottery. In order to stay in the country, Aditya had to enroll in another college degree program, after having obtained his master's degree only a year earlier.

There are also stories with happier endings. Devi Prasad Gorrepati, a successful international student from India, joined a firm called Mentor Graphics as a Corporate Applications Engineer after graduating as a mechanical engineer. After two failed attempts to secure his visa, the stars finally aligned for Devi in 2018—his last chance to participate in the H-1B visa lottery. Since Devi was a STEM major, his employer benefited from being able to file for his H-1B application three times. A super-proactive international student, Devi told me he had already started working on a back-up plan, which for him included the option to immigrate to Canada and pursue permanent residency there. I'm so glad he succeeded in the United States, however. Besides being bright, he also was involved in helping internationals get hired while he was still looking for a job himself.

And then there's Vishnu Sudha Vasu Mallipudi, an international computer science graduate I briefly met when I visited Sacred Heart University. Once Vishnu found his rhythm as a job seeker, the once-distant idea of working for a top technology employer did not seem so crazy anymore. Being able to identify the strong points that differentiated him from his competition was critical to Vishnu's win. The final result? A great job with Microsoft after graduation.

And finally there's Lana Do, an industrial engineering major from Vietnam who graduated from the University of Illinois Urbana Champaign in 2018. When Lana first reached out about her lack of job-search results, she sounded nervous but not quite ready to commit to a rigorous job-training program that might give her a better chance. When we spoke again several months later, I immediately sensed that her mindset had changed and knew she was ready to train like an Olympian and do the required work to get noticed and hired. She engaged with professionals in her field of interest—supply chain/e-commerce—who enthusiastically connected her with their networks of peers and colleagues. Whether she was conversing with employees at large or small companies, the results were the same: people were delighted with her qualifications. How do I know? Because I spoke with those who spoke with Lana.

It is true that Lana's profile was unusually strong and needed only minor tweaks to get the attention of prospective employers. What was most interesting, and what delighted me the most, was the meaningful transformation I witnessed. I saw Lana commit to running the job-search race with speed and purpose.

She wanted to win.

She wanted to leave a mark on the world.

She knew her dreams and goals were attainable.

Lana's success reminds us what is possible for career-driven international students. I did not need to tell Lana how to job search. It was enough to let her know what she was capable of and let her surprise me with her results.

In the end, Lana accepted a position at EME Technologies as an Industrial Engineer in Santa Clara, CA.

What's the Right Message for International Students?

Here's question I am often asked these days: "Has your message to international students who want to work in the United States changed since this book was first published in 2015?

The short answer is "no," though it is important to add a caveat. Whether I am working with international students enrolled at renowned universities or with students attending lesser-known programs, I find myself essentially training international students to acknowledge, honor, and confidently showcase their pre-U.S. strengths as key tools for solving complex challenges American employers face. The creative and distinctive thinking that international minds are capable of is only one of the many traits U.S. employers need, want, and cannot easily find.

We are all products of our environment. Helping international students become unstoppable job seekers starts by teaching them to leverage the gifts of their backgrounds. Harnessing the full power of the multicultural brain is what we aim for.

It's Your Decision

If, despite uncertainties that may be greater than ever, you do decide to run the job-search race as an international student with an eye on U.S. employment, then *The International Advantage* will run this race with you, from beginning to end. We want to equip you with the tools, data, and information you will need to beat the odds. The goal of *The International Advantage* program has never been to simply assist international students in managing their job-search challenges and help them secure visas. Ultimately, what we truly want is to see international minds explode professionally.

When international students find themselves in trouble and contact me for job-search help, they often ask me to review their resumes. That's not what I'm interested in. A question I ask is, "What does your typical day look like?" If someone says, "I get up at six, hit the gym, go to class, go to my job, complete group projects, do my homework until eleven, connect with five new people every day on LinkedIn, and in between apply for jobs that maximize my strengths," then I know that student has a chance.

Are you ready to get noticed and hired? Are you ready to get out of bed a little earlier to train harder? If you are, let's go!

INTRODUCTION

For as long as she could remember, Fang Wang had her mind set on going to the United States for college. The image of herself living abroad appealed to her—independent, intelligent, a global young woman full of potential. An MBA degree from an American university was only part of the attraction of studying overseas: the ultimate goal was to move her career forward and experience life in the United States as a working professional. She wanted a job in the United States. She was seeking more than an academic experience. Fang Wang wasn't ready to go back home after graduation. She had been studying English for years; though her language skills weren't great, they were better than those of most of the Chinese students I had worked with. Originally from Changsha, Hunan Province, the 23-year-old had high expectations for herself but lacked a basic understanding of how to create a job-search strategy that would allow her to achieve her goals. She was looking for guidance. That was a good start. Actually, that was an excellent start. When she came to me for help, however, I was unsure about her odds.

Like Fang Wang, each year, thousands of international students take the plunge and come to the United States for college, many believing they will beat the odds and find work in the United States after graduation by securing the coveted H-1B[1] visa. Despite the known challenges for

---

[1] To work in the United States after graduation, international students—usually F-1 or J-1 visa holders —must find an employer willing to sponsor them and file a petition with the U.S. government for an H-1B visa. International students cannot apply for an H-1B visa themselves. U.S. companies can also use the visa to hire someone who is outside of the United States and move him or her to a branch in the United States.

job seekers who need a work visa to remain in the United States after graduation, the United States maintains its position as the global hub of academic training. It hosts more international students than any other country in the world. According to "Open Doors," a report produced by the Institute of International Education, the nation's leading not-for-profit educational and cultural exchange organization, 948,519 international students were enrolled in U.S. universities during the 2021/2022 academic year.

Travel of any kind has the potential to deeply transform us, particularly when we approach it with an open mind and a hungry determination to understand what is new and different. The time Steve Jobs spent in India deeply shaped how he lived his life *and* how he approached his work. Jobs selected a book to be given out to those attending his funeral called *Autobiography of a Yogi*. This book focuses on the role of intuitions in our lives, a concept Jobs became familiar with during his travels in rural parts of India.

Going to college abroad will have a long-lasting impact on your life as well. The precious opportunity to attend college overseas will give you a new personal dimension and another view of the world. As an international student, you are now part of a very small group of people who went abroad to pursue a different type of educational experience. If you've been accepted into a U.S. college, you're already successful. Your international experience will become part of your identity: you'll see the world through a new lens. What a gift! You may learn that that your old way of making sense of the world is not the only way.

A good dose of persistence is incredibly important for international students seeking work in the United States. The amount of mental energy that goes into being an international student pursuing a college degree while managing a job search is incredible, particularly for students from non-English-speaking countries. International brains never take a break; they're constantly trying to process and decode—or "culturally translate"—everything happening around them.

From a career development standpoint, as an international student you hope doors will open up for you both professionally and socially due to your travels, your new experiences, and the weight of your U.S. college degree on your resume. You're probably worried, though, about whether you will find a job in the United States or have to return home after graduation. Many international students are seeking more than an academic experience. For many, a job in the United States after graduation is the ultimate prize. It may be the reason they decided to pursue a college degree in the United States in the first place. Anxiety about career advancement is an unavoidable part of the journey. The million-dollar question is: like Fang Wang, if you intend to stay in the United States and work after graduation, will you be able to convince an employer to hire you?

Challenges Beyond Visas

If you know anything about U.S. history (and you *should* study U.S. history if you're serious about staying in the United States for the long term), you know it is marked by groups of immigrants who brought their own dreams, cultures, and traditions to the United States, much the same way many international students today dream of a better future in the United States after graduation. This diversity of people from all over the world makes America the beautiful country it is today. But when it comes to hiring those who need a work visa, such as international students, this enthusiasm toward immigrants can quickly fade.

One of the hardest aspects of finding a job in the United States as an international student is the reluctance many U.S. employers have about hiring non-U.S. citizens. Navigating visa matters and dealing with companies' resistance to sponsoring are, without question, major barriers.

9

Chapter 12, "The Big, Bad Visa Chapter," focuses on this topic with an emphasis on highlighting clear benefits available via the H-1B visa program - it's not all bad news - that international job seekers should be excited about and incorporate into their job-search strategy.

Chapter 2, "What Employers Really Think about International Students," explains the unwillingness some companies may feel toward sponsoring so you can be prepared to manage these situations. Understanding how employers think is one of the first steps toward building a successful job-search campaign.

There are additional obstacles along the way, some that may be invisible to outsiders and some that might be invisible to international students themselves; all must be taken just as seriously, if not more seriously, than visa challenges. For example, many international students don't know how to spontaneously approach alumni during a networking event. When they eventually build up the courage to speak with someone, they often feel the need to "sell" themselves. Unsure how to network, many international students simply don't, preferring the safety of sitting behind a computer and applying for jobs online. Chapter 5, "Networking," provides a simple, effective framework for successful interactions that you'll actually enjoy implementing. This chapter is filled with examples that will immediately make sense for globally minded individuals.

Blindsided and confused by a hiring culture that does not always value good grades, international students often find that understanding the elusive hiring criteria required for certain jobs, like "fit," is tricky. What do American employers really value? When it comes to the job-search process, international students often don't understand the criteria by which their performance is being measured. Despite the job requirements stated in a job description, what U.S. employers may be looking for in a candidate is not always disclosed. In Chapter 7, we'll demystify what the term "fit" means and provide clear recommendations for how you can show U.S. employers that you not only "fit" but also bring more to the table. U.S. recruiters want to hire candidates who give them more than what they were initially looking for in their new hire. They also want to hire individuals who have taken courageous and interesting routes in their lives. International students are well positioned to meet these standards.

Waiting for companies that might be open to interviewing international students to come to your university cannot be your only job-search strategy. Many international students report very low levels of on-campus interview opportunities. More work will be required. Creative strategies will be needed not only to secure interviews but to succeed in interviews as well. Differentiated tactics that international students are comfortable executing are key. Chapter 10, "Interviewing," covers the conclusion of Fang Wang's U.S. job-search journey, particularly her interview preparation, which ultimately led to a great H-1B job. Her success is a reminder about what is possible when international students find themselves in their element.

Take Control

I am going to guide you through the aspects of the job-search process that I have seen international students struggle with most often, such as correctly engaging with your university career services center, preparing interview strategies you can execute with confidence, and smartly selecting target companies. All this, when handled correctly, will help you get closer to securing the job you want. Being aware of common job-search pitfalls that international students face is the first step toward avoiding them, and one of the goals of this book is to illuminate these key challenges.

Whether you're getting an MBA, a computer science degree, or an engineering degree; and regardless of whether you're a graduate or undergraduate international student looking for an H-1B job or thinking about what careers may best fit you—this book is for you. My intention is to focus on the commonalities that tend to unite all international job seekers. There are plenty.

I Know What It Feels Like

This is what I often hear from international students: "It's tough to be an international student. Most companies don't even give us a chance to interview." Such comments remind me of my own days as an international student, when I wanted exactly the same thing: a chance to compete. In Chapter 19, "Confessions of an International Career Coach," you will learn more about my own journey as an insecure international with big dreams of finding a great H-1B job after graduation.

How This Book Will Help

10-Pound Weight Drop in Two Weeks
4 Weeks to Your Beach Body by Eating Just Soup
Lose 30 Pounds FAST
Drop Five Sizes in Less than a Month

These are real headlines from magazine articles. Many people are drawn to them—unrealistic as they are—because they want to believe that someone out there, some expert, has finally figured out how to help them achieve great results quickly, without much hard work or commitment. You probably know where I'm going with this: I often say that the solution to the job-search challenges of international students seeking a job in the United States is not a click away. There's no magic spell, no secret job-search formula, no website or hidden database of H-1B jobs that are open to international students and match your interests. For good reason, this book is not called How to Secure Your H-1B Job in 30 Days.

The chance to compete for quality H-1B jobs does exist, but it often requires international students to abandon ineffective job-search strategies, such as applying for jobs online. There are clear ways to secure a great job in the United States as an international job seeker, no matter what university you go to, how experienced or inexperienced you are, or what type of job you decide to pursue. The possibility is real—which is why I'm motivated to help you achieve this goal. To overcome job-search obstacles, you must carefully manage each phase of the job-search marathon and ensure you don't fall behind.

On the surface, what international students need to do to secure a job may not seem tremendously different from what U.S. students need to do. Everybody needs to find their passion, network, interview, market themselves, and apply for the right types of jobs.

The unique challenges and opportunities that lie ahead for international job seekers call for differentiated job-search approaches.

To start, international students need to replace traditional job-search formulas that don't accommodate them with strategies that fit them. Fully capitalizing on the opportunities ahead is critical. The unique traits and characteristics international students possess allow them to take the conversations they have with U.S. recruiters, hiring managers, and contacts to a different level and wow those they talk to with their charm, intelligence, and world views. Chapter 5, "Networking," and Chapter 6, "Sharing Your Story," will focus on those ideas. Some methods that may initially appear slightly unconventional really aren't when you study them more closely.

If only I did not have an accent.
If only I did not need a visa.
If only employers would interview me.

The unique job search challenges international students often face can be converted into opportunities not available to other job seekers. While often difficult and long, the job-search process for international students can be transformational and yield long-lasting insights into who you are, your strengths, how others perceive you, and country-specific skills and traits your culture has given you that can get you hired. All of this is within reach. And such is the main goal of this book: to prove to you that as an international student you have powerful job search advantages that others don't. Even your initial lack of knowledge about how to conduct an effective U.S. job search, your lack of contacts in the United States, and your anxiety about returning home after graduation can all ultimately help you secure a great H-1B job.

International students may not necessarily be underdogs in the job-hunting race. As an American student once told me, in many ways international students have clear advantages when job searching. "Some international students have a real knack for turning data into intelligent business insight. They make it look so easy," he said. "Besides, they work so hard! I'd want to hire them." The intelligence international students are often known for is only the tip of the iceberg. Success is possible. Your unique value, skills, and profile are hard to find and are in demand.

By picking up this book, you've already shown yourself to be a capable, responsible individual who wants to take charge of your future. Regarding how to get the most out of *The International Advantage*, start anywhere. If you have an interview coming up, go straight to Chapter 10, "Interviewing On Your Terms", to get some ideas that might help you. If you will be attending a business function soon where you will be meeting new people, jump to Chapter 5, "Become a Global Networker." Engage with the content along the way. Take notes. Underline critical concepts and frameworks as you read.

Good planning coupled with creative and steady execution, as well as some luck, can help you secure a great H-1B job. Many before you have done it. Now it is your turn. If you want something to happen, make it happen. Never has the world been smaller, and never has there been a greater need for U.S. employers to hire candidates with the traits that international students have but sometimes take for granted. So this is where we're headed. I'm ready to embark on this journey with you. Let's get going!

1

GETTING THE MOST OUT OF CAREER SERVICES

Many international students are not thinking about what career suits them best or what jobs to apply for once they arrive in the United States. As newcomers to a new country, many are more concerned with improving their language skills, figuring out how to make friends with Americans, traveling, and getting good grades. The desire to stay and work may develop over time for some, while others know from day one that they want to stay in the U.S after graduation.

Regardless of your motivation for becoming an international student, one of the biggest benefits available to you is the chance to acquire valuable job-searching skills. Studying at a U.S. university provides you with a unique opportunity to receive great help with career matters from professionals who are trained to help you answer one of the greatest questions of all time: what should I do with my life? This type of specialized help may not be available in your home country, so it makes sense to leverage it before you graduate, regardless of whether you plan to seek work in the United States or wish to return home. Job-hunting can be hard for anyone, and it can be particularly difficult for international students. Fortunately, you have access to a great deal of help, help that is sometimes geared toward the unique job-search needs of international students.

Many international students come from countries where going to college is primarily about taking classes; apart from professors and perhaps a few support staff, not many people interact with students regularly. In many countries, students select a major prior to entering college. Higher education in the United States is structured differently. Besides professors, many other individuals work directly with students, and they are often tasked with the business of making you successful. This is terrific news for international students interested in securing a job in the United States.

When the time comes to consider a major, or if you're wondering how to get an internship or an H-1B job after graduation, key support comes from career services. Most students—domestic and international—don't realize what a gift it is to have easy, "free"[1] access to career services. Specialized help with career matters is one of the most attractive characteristics of higher education in the United States in my opinion. Your journey toward securing an H-1B job must start at your university's career center. The main challenge for many international students is that many have never worked with a career coach before; the concept may not mean much to them. They are unsure how to utilize their university's career center. Similarly, confusion regarding what to expect—and not expect —from career services remains a problem for international students. I have had students tell me after graduation that they wished I had better explained to them what a career center does, why it exists, and what it is *not*. This is the reason for this chapter.

---

[1] Your university tuition covers access to career services, so technically you're not spending extra money to sit down with a career coach to evaluate suitable career options. Take advantage of this great opportunity.

The Great Unknowns

Career issues are particularly complex for international students because they are trying to answer a critical question—What should I do with my life?—outside of their element. Even if you are lucky enough to know what type of career fits you, you may be clueless about the practicalities of finding jobs in the field you're interested in. You don't know what you don't know as an international job seeker, but there is help available. While you may not initially understand the mysterious hiring criteria that nobody directly talks about that you will need to know to secure the jobs you want, if you engage with career services, the mystery can go away. Fully leveraging the services provided by your university's career center is essential! Your job-search journey will be less stressful and more productive and predictable when you partner with career services.

Cover the Basics

I occasionally get contacted by international students from schools around the United States who are looking to get some help with their job search. Whenever possible, I enjoy taking the time to speak with these students, as I always learn a great deal myself. I listen attentively to the kinds of questions students have. In many cases, the questions I receive are basic and clearly indicate that the student has not engaged with career services. In these situations, I always ask the students when they last spoke with a career counselor. In many instances I have heard, "I never have." That's a problem on several different levels. In the professional world, time is of the essence, and nobody wants to find themselves answering basic questions that could have been investigated and resolved with readily available help. Recruiters feel the same way. A recruiter for a well-known Big 4 firm came to the university where I worked to present information about job opportunities at her firm. Since this firm sponsored, the session was well attended by international students. After the session, the recruiter told me that several international students had approached her with basic questions about the job-search process, such as how to create a strong resume or how to best prepare to interview with her. Her response was always the same, she later told me: "This is something your career center can help you with." The first impressions these students made on the recruiter left a lot to be desired. Don't make the same mistake. Leverage your university's career center so when you speak with recruiters and hiring managers they immediately feel you're well prepared. This is a great way to make a great first impression.

Priorities and Patience

Over the years, I have casually asked many international students why they had not engaged with their career centers. A few of the most common responses I've received are:

- "My career center doesn't have jobs open for international students."

- "I'm not looking for a job in the United States, so why should I go to my university's career center?"

- "No companies coming to campus that interest me are open to hiring international students."

- "I've been too busy with classes. I don't have time."

- "The career coach I talked to did not understand my job-search needs as an international student."

- "I went to career services once and didn't get enough value, so I stopped going."

Let me say this first: don't expect things to happen too fast. Your job is to remain engaged with your career center throughout your studies in the United States.

You may come from a country where your university career center primarily focuses on bringing firms to campus to hire you. Depending on where you come from, you may not receive much help polishing your interviewing skills, or learning how to correctly interact with people. Similarly, you may not receive assistance understanding what careers and jobs are best for you, and which ones are not. On-campus recruiting is certainly a key feature offered by Career Centers at U.S. universities but it is only one of many services provided. One of my goals in writing this book is to empower you to go after the job you deserve—and that means getting off campus, and not overly relying on your career center to bring a firm to your school that you like and is willing to interview you. Use your university on-campus recruiting as a way to complement your job search efforts.

Manage your expectations carefully so you remain motivated to develop a strong working relationship with a career advisor. Ultimately, you own your job search, but career advisors are eager to assist and they love to see international students succeed. Career centers cannot guarantee you a job, though; this is not their role. But they are rooting for you, and their staff has the training and experience to best prepare you to achieve your goals. In fact, given the large increase of international students enrolled in U.S. universities, some career centers have professionals on staff focused on addressing the specific job search needs of international students. This is excellent news, isn't it?

Regarding the common complaint from international students that not many companies willing to interview them are coming to campus, the ability of career centers to convince employers to interview international students is limited. You'll learn later why this is the case.

What Career Advisors Can Do to Help International Students

Your career advisor can be a strong ally in your quest to achieve your job-search goals. He or she will be able to offer or suggest:

- Assessments that help you better understand yourself and career paths that might be suitable for you.

- Job leads and alumni contacts, including international alumni from your country who got jobs in the United States.

- Helpful services and workshops, sometimes especially designed for international students.

- Information on companies you haven't heard about that sponsor international students.

- Job-search strategies that address visa challenges.

- Global career paths that you may not have considered.

- Individualized coaching sessions that may help you recognize the skills and unique qualities you developed before coming to the United States.

No matter what it is you're thinking of pursuing—engineering, math, computer science, business, or literature—explore the world of U.S. jobs and careers with an open mind. If you do so, you will quickly come to see just how fluid this world is.

Your relationship with a career advisor will be valuable both short-term and long-term. He or she will ensure that your priorities are in order, hold you accountable for achieving your goals, and help celebrate your success. While this book will help you a great deal, it does not at all replace the assistance of a career coach who can recognize your personal strengths, weaknesses, and the particular areas that could cause you trouble during your job search. You'll need help creating a customized job-search strategy that takes into account your uniqueness as well as the typical challenges you're likely to face. I've written this book with the idea that you'll be implementing these recommendations while working alongside a career advisor.

The Questions to Ask

There are many great questions you can ask your career advisor, though the direction your discussions with an advisor will take will vary depending on your background, goals, and job targets. Here are a few questions that might serve as a jumping-off point:

What career paths and job opportunities might be available for someone with my interests?

This is a crucial question. Given what you know about yourself and your interests - maybe you love Math and solving problems in general - work with your advisor to identify job opportunities and career paths that exploit opportunities in the U.S. marketplace that could lead to a good H-1B job after graduation.

Start broad. While U.S students have virtually no restrictions on the jobs they can apply for, international students do not enjoy a comparable freedom. You might be able to create a bigger pool of job opportunities that fit your profile and career interests if you initially take a big-picture view of what career paths might be available to you.

You may already have knowledge and skills that can be applied in multiple fields.

Besides, by exploring multiple potential career paths and majors that look interesting with an open mind, you will be able to confidently rule out choices you couldn't before.

An international student who knows which jobs to target may ask their career coach the following question: "I know I want to manage databases. Do you have any database administrator job leads that are open to international students?" The "problem" with this question is that it does not offer much room for interesting dialogue or exploration. Early in your job search, prioritize learning about interesting career options that you might not have considered or perhaps don't even know about. A better question is: "What possible career paths might be available for someone with an interest in database management? See the difference?

Here is another good way to open a discussion with your advisor:

> *I've been so busy adjusting to classes and life in the United States that I've neglected my job-search efforts entirely. Help me get organized, please. I'm ready to focus.*

This is a perfectly acceptable statement! It is very common for international students to feel overwhelmed and unsure about how to start their job search, and career-center professionals are certainly aware of this challenge. It is completely fine to let your career coach know that you're confused and unsure what to do, and that you feel you're falling behind. Your honesty and courage will earn your career advisor's respect and you will understand why that is when you read Chapter 5, "Networking". Career-center professionals know how tough it can be for international students. Not seeking help is the biggest mistake of all. Never feel like you need to impress your career advisor. Your advisor will help you navigate the job-search process, provide structure, share valuable resources, ask you lots of questions, and help you develop strong job searching skills. Your career advisor is not there to judge you or grade you. Try to overcome cultural barriers and get into the habit of sharing with your advisor your thoughts about your career goals and job-search difficulties.

Here is another good question you can ask your career advisor:

> *Given my profile (strengths and weaknesses) and my career interests and goals, how often do you recommend that I meet with you in order to stay on track?*

Understanding how often you should meet with your career advisor is key to successfully starting the journey of achieving your job-search goals. If months go by and you don't meet with your advisor, don't be too worried: schedule an appointment and re-engage. One of the best investments you can make is developing a trusting and productive working relationship with your career advisor. For that to occur, on-going contact between you and your advisor is needed. Besides, if a job lead comes into your career services center with requirements that match your profile and interests, your advisor may not think of you if you haven't taken the time to build up the relationship.

Of course, one of the basic elements of an effective job-search strategy is a clear understanding of what you want, coupled with a realistic assessment of your strengths and weaknesses. When determining what skill gaps you may have, or what abilities you should aggressively market, an outside perspective is key, and your career advisor may have some insight for you. If not, he or she may know someone in your field of interest with whom you can talk. A good question to ask your advisor and those you meet with is:

What gaps do you see in my profile in terms of skills or experience that you think I must try to address in order to increase my chances of securing an H-1B job?

Be a confident job seeker who is aware of gaps in your profile and work history. Work with your advisor to design a plan to help you close these gaps if it makes sense to do so.

Similarly, ask your mentors and those who work in the field you're trying to break into this question:

Could you please tell me what you think are the two biggest weaknesses in my profile?

Ask the "right questions"—be specific—so you can get the data you need to improve. You don't want to hear only what you do well, though that is most critical. Collect data about areas of improvement as well so you know what your weak spots are. If you ask the wrong questions, you won't get the right answers.

Speaking of strengths and weaknesses, what's more important: learning about your weaknesses and working hard to fix them or learning about your strengths? The correct answer may surprise you: prioritize learning about your strengths! Employers are buying your strengths. They want to know what you can do well and what comes naturally to you. U.S. employers are more interested in how your strengths will help their firms grow than learning about your weaknesses. Chapter 13, "Nail the Basics: Job-Search Strategies You Must Use," will address in detail how international students can speak about their strengths. Honoring your strengths as an international student can be challenging but will be key to your success.

Finally, your career advisor is probably an intensely curious human being. Why not take a little bit of time to share with him or her who you are, why you decided to come to the United States for college, and maybe even how your culture has shaped you? When you feel comfortable telling your personal story to others, you will start interacting with people on a whole different level, as you'll learn in Chapter 5, "Networking." A safe way to start doing this is to talk with your career advisor, particularly in the very early stages of building a relationship with him or her. Give it a try.

In summary, ask your career advisor broad questions that expand your awareness about yourself and career goals and also start introducing you to different strategies you can utilize to secure your H-1B job.

Career Centers Are in Your Corner

Career centers across the country have tried to promote the unique characteristics that international students bring to the table. Here is a selection of enthusiastic statements collected from university career centers websites nationwide:

"Because of the special abilities and cultural experiences they possess, international students can be ideally suited for employment within the American workforce, and the Pomerantz Career Center encourages prospective employers to consider them carefully when recruiting."

The University of Iowa

"International students bring cross-cultural communication and multicultural perspective to the workplace, in addition to the knowledge gained from their studies at GW."

The George Washington University

"Luther College is blessed to enroll a very talented group of international students. In total, more than 100 international students from across the globe attend Luther. They complement the campus community with very rich and diverse life experiences, strong analytical and problem-solving skills, and often times advanced proficiency with multiple languages."

Luther College

"International students are an extraordinary addition to any company. At Harvard Business School they represent over a third of the MBA population and come from more than 70 countries. In an increasingly global marketplace, competitive organizations are pursuing global competency as a key attribute in their hiring so this is a pool of talented professionals you should not overlook."

Harvard Business School

"Opening opportunities to international students will considerably broaden your pool of exceptional candidates."

Stanford Graduate School of Business

The statement below does not come from a university career center, but it is very interesting as well. Take a look:

"Globalization is causing policy and business leaders to call for new competencies to advance U.S. competitiveness, leadership in global markets, scientific innovation, security, and proactively improve international relations...These new realities demonstrate that future workers seeking careers in business, government, health care, law enforcement, and a wide variety of other jobs will all require global knowledge and skills."

Excerpted from Michael H. Levine (Progressive Policy Institute), "Putting the World into Our Classrooms: A New Vision for 31st Century Education," April 2005

In spite of the efforts of universities to promote international students to employers, at the end of the day, you may have heard that many doors are closed to international students who seek jobs that require sponsorship. Understanding why is the first step to creating job-search strategies that will increase your chances of securing your H-1B job.

2

What Employers Think About International Students

Let's get the bad news out of the way fast. Despite universities' efforts to promote international students to employers, a large number of U.S. job descriptions still contain language like this: "Applications from individuals with a non-immigrant visa (i.e., F-1 or J-1) who are not eligible to work permanently in the United States are not accepted." In other words, if you need sponsorship, you're out. And yes, it is completely legal for employers to specify that they are not interested in interviewing those who need work authorization, such as international students.

Less-than-friendly work visa regulations have made it difficult for undecided companies to move forward with the idea of considering hiring workers who need a work visa. International students can be perceived as difficult to work with because of the bureaucracy, cost, and risk that go along with hiring someone who needs an H-1B. Companies need to spend money to try to secure an H-1B visa for an international hire. They have to work with an attorney to fill out forms, and they have to meet filing deadlines. In general, they don't like to do any of that. Companies usually like easy and simple when it comes to hiring. At the end of the day, firms have to be lucky, too: there are no guarantees that they will be able to obtain an H-1B visa for you and keep you as an employee, because lately the demand for H-1B visas has surpassed the number of visas available[1]. Some companies that would genuinely like to give international students a try are frustrated by the perceived hassle of working with hires that need an H-1B visa.

And to top it all off, in a slowing economy, employers feel they are likely to find a U.S. citizen with the skill set they *think* they need for a particular job, so a supply-and-demand approach seems to be used by many.

Understanding an Organization's Recruitment Strategy

When I hear from international students that U.S. companies don't want to hire them, I go through a quick exercise of "correcting" what they say. I tell them, "I think there's a slightly different way for you to say what you just said." Many U.S. employers seem to *think* they don't need to hire international students, so they choose not to interview them. It's a rational decision on their part. It *appears* to be the right thing for them to do, I continue, but is it? What do they lose if they don't hire *you*?

Justifications

Frequent interactions with recruiters over the years provided me with many opportunities to gather views regarding the hiring climate for international students and those without permanent work authorizations.

What follows are some of the common statements I have heard from employers when I've tried to gauge their appetite for hiring international students:

---

[1] This mismatch of supply and demand for H-1B visas creates uncertainties for HR departments. For fiscal year 2023, the United States Citizenship and Immigration Services (USCIS) received 483,927 applications for a possible 85,000 H-1B visas. Do you see the huge supply and demand imbalance? But don't get discouraged. There are ways to increase your odds. Chapter 12, "The Big, The Bad Visa Chapter Under Trump" will outline specific strategies you can utilize.

- "We have a policy in place not to hire international students, and we don't make any exceptions."

- "We only consider international students for IT roles."

- "If they knock our socks off—if they are exceptional—yes, we will consider hiring them. It's case-by-case for us."

- "We do hire international students. Our interview schedule should have been open to international students from the start. We probably just made a mistake."

- "We don't want to worry about having to prove to the U.S. government that no U.S. citizen was available for the job." (*Note: This is a BIG misconception. Such proof is not a requirement for an H-1B petition.*)

- "I was unsure of my company policy regarding whether or not we hire international students when I called your office, so I thought it was best not to interview them, to be on the safe side."

- "We'd really like to consider international students, but the current visa situation makes it difficult for us to do so."

- "We hire international students occasionally but prefer not to advertise that so we don't get flooded with a ton of international resumes"

Clearly, employers have different justifications for their desire—or lack thereof—to hire international students. Some are confused about what they can and cannot do, and may need to be educated by you or your university. Others completely understand the hiring process for international students and simply choose not to explore this option. You have to be aware of the various justifications so you can appropriately address them during your job search, *when possible*. For undecided or confused employers—or perhaps firms without much experience with sponsorship—you may have a great opportunity to show them that it is possible for them to hire you. Chapter 12, "The Big, Bad Visa Chapter," will provide you with examples and templates of just what to say to calm employers down, ease their anxiety, and encourage them to hire you.

It's a Little Tough Out There, but You Can Succeed

You have a lot of dreams as an international student. A job with Microsoft, Amazon, or Google probably sounds great to you. You are talented and hardworking, and you are spending a lot of money to go to college in the United States. Sometimes there's a lot at stake. Keep in mind that employers, especially well-known firms, get many resumes these days, and they have the luxury of choosing from countless excellent candidates, some of whom may have worked for their competitors in a role identical to the open job.

Employers care about *their* goals and needs first, and then yours.

As an international job seeker in the United States, put yourself in the shoes of prospective employers and get used to trying to see the world from their point of view. Put their needs ahead of yours initially, because they hold much more power in the job-search game.

Top Performance

International students make great workers and bring much needed creativity to American organizations. When surveyed, U.S. employers found that recent hires with international experience stood out and excelled *beyond their peers* in these areas:

- Interacting with people who hold different interests, values, or perspectives

- Understanding cultural differences in the workplace

- Adapting to situations of change

- Gaining new knowledge from experiences

- Ability to work independently

- Undertaking tasks that are unfamiliar/risky

- Applying information in new or broader contexts

- Identifying new problems/solutions to problems

- Working effectively with coworkers

When you review the list above, do you feel you have some of the same characteristics and abilities? Chances are you do. Make an initial list of how your background has shaped you and how it sets you apart from U.S. students. Some differences are quite obvious: perhaps you're multilingual; perhaps working in your home country has taught you to adapt to particular political or economic circumstances; or perhaps your experience as an international student has helped you to relate to and work with people from many different cultures. Start brainstorming specific examples from your previous work and academic experiences that reflect the areas listed above.

In addition, take a look at the quotes below from U.S. employers. Do you believe you have these characteristics? As they say in the United States, do you fit the bill?

"All major hiring companies need global citizens. Global sensitivities, global perspective, global insight, along with maturity and a capacity for risk-taking, are exactly the skills every major organization is looking for—in every industry."

Kevin Gill, Global Director of Staffing for Honeywell

"In this era of globalization, with the increasing cross-border reach of business and regulators, tax issues are seldom purely local in nature. This means tax advisors must be prepared to 'think global to act local'—on behalf of clients large and small."

Greg Wiebe, Global Head of Tax for KPMG

"In the financial world, cultural awareness and cultural adeptness are far more important than undergraduate major or existing skill sets…These needs touch all industries, from banking to healthcare to engineering."

Jonathan Jones, Firmwide Campus Recruiting Director for
Goldman Sachs

Studying Abroad Stands Out

Some international students secure good jobs in the United States after graduation because they can reflect on their experiences in the United States with depth, making it easy for employers to understand the unique value they bring. Their intellect, maturity, and likeability get them hired. The value gleaned from your experiences in the United States will only matter to American employers if you can link your experiences and traits to the target job's specific requirements, as well as to the overall mission of the firm you want to join. I am confident you will learn how to do this by the time you finish reading *The International Advantage.* In the process of doing this, you'll stand out and differentiate yourself from other candidates.

Other international students achieve career success in the United States because they possess skills and knowledge that are in demand by U.S. firms. With that in mind, let's take a close look at a special group of international students who are in a very good position to secure a great job in the United States after graduation.

3

IT'S GREAT TO BE AN
INTERNATIONAL STEM MAJOR

The U.S. economy does not seem to be generating enough workers to fill jobs that require high levels of knowledge in science, technology, engineering, and mathematics (STEM). Not enough American students are selecting STEM majors when they go to college. In theory, this trend benefits international STEM graduates who wish to find a job in the United States. What I'll present in this chapter is an initial answer to a question I've been asked again and again: what does it take to secure a great job in the United States after graduation as a non-U.S. citizen? While pursuing a STEM major is certainly not the only way to succeed, in-demand skills relating to information technology (IT) or mathematics, for example, will give you a true advantage.

The shortage of U.S. workers in STEM fields often forces companies to open jobs to international students as a way to fill their vacancies. Even better, the intense competition among companies to hire the few college grads who qualify for certain STEM roles causes salaries to go up. Recent graduates with a bachelor's degree in a non-STEM field earn less than their peers who pursued STEM degrees, particularly in the early stages of their careers. According to data compiled by Payscale.com for their 2017-2018 College Salary Report - Payscale.com is a site that allow users to compare their salaries - the median salary for alumni with a bachelor's degree and 0-5 years of work experience in jobs in high-demand STEM fields, such as petroleum engineering, chemical engineering, and actuarial science, for instance, pay north of $60,000 per year. In fact, language in the job description of certain STEM positions makes it very clear that H-1B visa seekers should apply. What a luxury.

As a friend of mine puts it, exotic majors are in demand and deserve careful consideration from international students who may wish to establish themselves permanently in the U.S after graduation. Certain STEM fields might be more international student friendly than others though. For example, many international students report that Aerospace Engineering is an extremely difficult field for international students to break into due to the common requirement of firms in this space to only consider U.S. citizens as candidates. Remember to do your research, choose carefully, and understand that your choice of major can have an even bigger impact in your ability to stay and work in the United States after graduation than your choice of school.

STEM majors are considered "tough majors," and that works out well for many international students, who are used to studying hard and have the mental discipline needed to perform well academically under pressure. International students from Asian countries, for example, come from educational systems grounded in the rigor of science- and math-related disciplines, which prepares them to pursue a STEM degree in the United States. Strong academic performance in a STEM major boosts the self-esteem and confidence of international students who wish to stay and work in the United States. Employers interested in STEM majors generally look for candidates with current knowledge of the technologies and statistical packages needed to perform well in the field they choose. Research and data analysis skills will be in demand as well. According to the "Open Doors"[1] report, about 49% of international students attending college in the United States every year pick a STEM major.

You'll enjoy excellent benefits when job searching as an international STEM major—benefits that aren't available to international students pursuing non-STEM degrees. The U.S. government has responded to the scarcity of qualified workers in STEM fields by providing longer periods of Optional Practical Training[2] (OPT) work authorizations. STEM graduates enjoy 36 months of OPT versus the standard 12 months that non-STEM majors have. The additional 24 months of OPT extension only available to STEM majors provides great relief to employers. In fact, it is worth gold. The extension allows your employer to possibly petition for an H-1B visa on your behalf three times, in three successive fiscal years, as long as you remain on OPT. So if you don't get lucky your first time around you can try again the following year. This is a huge benefit for your employer, because it essentially triples your chance of securing an H-1B, compared to non-STEM majors who often only have only one shot at securing their visa.

One could say that international STEM majors are allowed easier access to the U.S. job market compared to non-STEM majors.

If you are an international STEM major, make sure potential employers clearly understand the value associated with the 24-month OPT extension. Essentially, what the U.S. government is saying is, "Mr. Employer,

---

[1] Open Doors is a report created by an organization called the Institute of International Education. Amongst other statistics, the report contains information regarding the typical majors international students choose when studying at U.S. universities.

[2] With OPT, international students are allowed to gain work experience related to their field of study in the United States after graduation. OPT usually comes before an H-1B. Students must find an employer willing to hire them as OPT workers.

I have made it very possible for you to hire international STEM majors so they can help your company grow."

U.S. employers seem to be taking advantage of the H-1B program to try to hire STEM graduates. In fact, almost two-thirds of requests for H-1B workers are for those with a STEM degree, with computer science graduates leading the pack. Other industries, such as healthcare, finance, business, and life sciences, are also in high demand, according to a 2012 Brookings Institution report[3].

Your Major: A Golden Ticket. Choose Carefully

These statistics suggest that international students who wish to work in the United States after graduation would be wise to study technical subjects in order to increase their chance of securing U.S. employment. International students with STEM degrees are strong contenders in the H-1B sponsorship race. They have much to look forward to, although there are never guarantees.

By the same logic, if your background, skills, or field of study is common or in high supply, then opportunities to interview may be more limited. Everything is possible, in theory, but international students *tend* to fare better when their skills fill a niche in the market that has a low supply of domestic candidates. If you are trying to improve your chance of staying in the United States after graduation, choosing a STEM major [4] has clear advantages. STEM majors are offered at both the undergraduate and graduate level at U.S. universities. If you don't pick a STEM major

---

[3] The Brookings Institution is a non-profit public-policy organization based in Washington, DC. In July 2012, they issued a report called "The Search for Skills: Demand for H-1B Immigrant Workers in U.S. Metropolitan Areas." The report is not a job-search guide for international students per se, but if you'd like to learn about the demand for H-1B workers in various parts of the United States, it is certainly worth a read. It can be accessed free of cost at www.brookings.edu/wp-content/uploads/2016/06/18-h1b-visas-labor-immigration.pdf

[4] For a list of majors that qualify as STEM refer to the following link: https://www.ice.gov/doclib/sevis/pdf/stemList2022.pdf

but possess STEM-like skills, such as is the case with many international MBAs, that can be powerful as well and should attract the attention of U.S. employers.

The shortage of STEM graduates in particular parts of the United States has caused some states to take action. Michigan seems to be the first U.S. state to create a program specifically designed to encourage local companies to recruit international students to work in the Detroit area. This program is called the Global Talent Retention Initiative of Southeast Michigan (GTRI). Companies in the Detroit area need to grow but often cannot find the right people to hire, particularly for STEM jobs. According to the GTRI website (www.migtri.org), "GTRI encourages employers to consider all qualified applicants, both domestic and foreign."

As if the aforementioned benefits of STEM majors were not enough, when the time comes for an employer to transition you from an H-1B worker to a green-card holder (*not* the focus of this book), STEM graduates may have a leg up due to their specific, in-demand hard skills. The shortage of qualified American workers willing or able to fill certain STEM jobs may make it easier down the road for an employer to prove to the U.S. government that no U.S. worker is available to fill your H-1B job, therefore increasing your chances of successfully obtaining permanent residency, which might be your ultimate goal as an international student.

Once again, if you end pursuing a non-STEM degree, take advantage of the flexibility of the U.S. educational system and take a few classes outside your major to enhance your profile, and acquire STEM skills that are in demand by U.S. employers and that might make you a more competitive job seeker. While it may be a great idea to enroll in some sort of "communications course" in order to improve your speaking and presentation skills since these skills are critical as you will learn in Chapter 9, "Communication Skills", you may also need to strengthen your profile by picking up some technology and data analytics skills, for example.

Passion Will Always Matter

Every report indicates that STEM graduates will continue to enjoy a strong job market in the United States, with IT and engineering graduates leading the pack. There's even better news: a quick Google search will reveal many reports that indicate global competition for STEM talent. For international STEM majors who are adventurous and highly mobile, opportunities for career success outside of the United States or their home countries may exist as well.

The technical and analytical skills that STEM majors often have lend themselves to a variety of jobs, sometimes in fields not directly related to their studies. This kind of information can be confusing for international students to interpret but it is not necessarily bad news. It speaks to how fluid the job market in the United States is, and how some U.S. employers don't place a huge emphasis on your undergraduate major. They want your skills, your value!

The choice of which major to pick becomes more important at the graduate level, as far as career advancement is concerned. Work with your career center and academic advisors to determine if your desired career aligns more closely with certain majors than others.

If you're overwhelmed by the endless choices of undergraduate majors at U.S. universities, pick something you like. Passion will always be key— for international students, for domestic students, for STEM majors, for non-STEM majors, for everybody. Never lose sight of that. If you love engineering, computer science, or a different STEM major, and you want to stay in the United States after graduation, great. But if you're drawn to business, literature, or journalism, or any other major that might seem impractical, don't despair. Technically, an H-1B visa is available for those who study any major.

If, after listening to your inner voice, you are still confused about what you want to focus on career-wise, don't worry. Don't get anxious if you don't have an immediate answer for what you want to do professionally. With so many majors and minors that may not exist in your home country, possible career paths; so much flexibility, and so many classes to choose from, it's easy to feel very overwhelmed. Your career center has professionals ready to help you determine your interests and passions. What gives you energy? Have you found something that you really want to learn more about? Interest is what drives people to invest time in developing the skills they need to become good at what they're doing. Many believe that you either have motivation or you don't. Employers hire motivated people, of course. They don't have to train these types of employees, because they end up training themselves.

Get into the habit of asking new U.S. acquaintances what they studied in college and how it relates to what they are doing professionally. Don't be surprised if you find philosophy majors who became computer programmers and now work on Wall Street, and computer science majors who became MBA career coaches. With the exception of medicine, law, and perhaps accounting, there often seems to be little correlation between Americans' careers and what they studied in college. Hart Research Associates, a firm which extensive experience with public opinion surveys, conducted a study to find out what American employers seek in college hires and they stated that 93% of U.S. employers who were surveyed agreed with this statement: "A candidate's demonstrated capacity to think critically, communicate clearly, and solve complex problems is more important than their undergraduate major."

You must have genuine interest in a field in order to be successful and find career fulfillment. Your innate strengths will guide your career success in your host country, at home, or anywhere in the world. The contacts you make during your job-search marathon need to be inspired by your honesty. If they are, they will be more inclined to help you achieve your goals.

NEVER give up on your dreams just because what you love seems impractical from a visa standpoint. When you embrace and accept your passion, you'll go further—despite the obstacles that will stand in your way. Your passions are going to give you the energy you need to run the job-search marathon. Pursue something that's real to you. You have to make this long race worth it.

4

THE IMPACT OF CULTURE

Whether we like it or not, we are all predisposed to behave and act in certain ways based on how our culture has shaped us. Culture impacts what clothes you feel comfortable wearing, how often you shower[1], the strength of your handshake, whether you're comfortable making eye contact with strangers, and a variety of other factors. Culture impacts how you react emotionally when an employer tells you it doesn't sponsor. Culture impacts how you interact with faculty, your teammates, recruiters, and your career advisor. Culture is very complex, and it will affect the job-search process in unexpected ways. Reviewing your own cultural values in relation to the cultural expectations of American employers must be an ongoing exercise.

Your university will probably provide you with some type of "cultural training" to help you function in America the "right way." You'll be taught the importance of having a firm handshake, smiling, and looking people in the eye when talking to them. At times, you may feel the message you're receiving is, "Act like us, because we feel more comfortable when you behave the way we do." Many advise international students to become more pragmatic and adjust. There's truth to that. While you

---

[1] When the Portuguese arrived in Brazil, they noticed that the natives bathed often in the region's abundant rivers. European settlers adopted this custom. To this day, we Brazilians love our showers. Understand the power of hygiene and know what American employers expect.

may need to be ready to speak, think, and behave in ways that might be considered rude under the rules you grew up with, look at this process of adaptation as a challenge, part of your international adventure.

Don't lose yourself along the way. Remain true to who you are, always, because that's always going to be your main advantage. In this chapter, we will address culture in a different way: as a key attribute that international students should leverage to achieve short- and long-term career success and fulfillment in the United States.

The Chance to Define Yourself

Living in the United States may give you a priceless opportunity: the chance to define who you are without the constraints of the culture in which you grew up, and perhaps the pressure from your parents telling you to become a doctor or an engineer, when you have no interest in either profession. The majority of international students don't even think about what they want. You may not have enjoyed such freedom growing up. But now, far away from it all, you're free to reinvent yourself, to discover your passions, and—maybe for the first time—to consider what you want to do with your life. The distance from home will allow you to be introspective, which is one of the many joys of traveling and studying overseas.

Loneliness is not unusual for international students to experience. Turn it into an opportunity to become extremely self-aware and create a level of emotional closeness with yourself that you might not have been able to experience in your home country. Away from common influences and distractions, you can develop an acute awareness of yourself and your surroundings. Perhaps for the first time, you can think about your strengths, weaknesses, where you fit, where you don't, the kind of job you'd love to have, and the kind of work you'd hate. Recruiters and hiring managers often report that they can quickly sense when a candidate is self-aware; this candidate immediately grabs their attention. Gather additional insights into your traits, strengths, and work style by seeking feedback from your peers and career coach. Don't be afraid to ask, "How do I come across? What have you noticed about my work style? What do you consider my strengths and weaknesses to be?" Always be very open to feedback.

Establishing a new professional identity for yourself—different from your parents' vision—just because you're far away from the familiar context and constraints of home isn't always as easy as it seems. Our culture shapes our values and expectations in every part of our lives, and we don't leave those behind when we live and study overseas.

One of the initial questions you need to ask yourself is whether your career choices are being influenced by the context of your new host country, your home country, or a combination of both. Share insights with your career advisor about the values and expectations of your own culture and how those might be influencing your career choices. This honest dialogue will strengthen your relationship with your advisor and improve his or her ability to help you. I guarantee that your career coach will love having this kind of conversation with you.

The Guilt Factor

In some cases, your culture can hold you back. If you're the only child of a traditional Asian family, for example, you may feel a moral responsibility to return home after graduation. Your parents may be saying, "Stay. Invest in your future. Don't worry about us." Despite their encouragement, you may still feel torn, because you're not completely comfortable with the idea of living away from family and pursuing your own dreams. You come from a place where you're expected to care for your parents as they age. Even though that expectation may have changed over the years, it's still not that easy for you to go away to pursue your own projects. Your parents want you to embrace exciting global opportunities that they may have dreamed of for themselves but were never available to them. But your culture may be whispering that moving far away and leaving your parents behind may not be the right thing to do. You're conflicted. There may be a struggle between a new self that wants to be independent and explore the world and an old self that may have been conditioned to be careful, respectful of cultural traditions, and obedient. You don't know how to deal with the guilt. If you stay, are you placing your own needs and desires ahead of your family's? These are just some of the unique challenges that international students face.

It's different for American students. Western culture often emphasizes individualism, and Americans have been taught from an early age to "fend for themselves" and "be all they can be." In some ways, career decisions can be more straightforward for them. They tend not to weigh their own goals and dreams against the goals of the community or group. They have been encouraged and conditioned to pursue jobs and educational opportunities that will better themselves, even if that means they'll be living thousands of miles away from their parents and seeing them only once or twice a year. Their culture does not hold them back in this regard. In fact, it gives them the "green light" to freely pursue their own dreams at full speed. They tend not to overthink these matters.

Culture and Your Job Search

Your culture may have instilled characteristics that might cause issues during your job search. For instance, if you realize that you're not very good at networking, or not very good at asking for help even though you've been told many times that it's okay to do so, it's important for you to consider *why* you're having these difficulties. Your difficulties may be grounded in a past you didn't ask for. You have to diagnose the problem correctly in order to address it successfully. Strive to understand your behavior and personality within the historical and cultural contexts of the place where you grew up, and then be patient with yourself. While adapting is important to succeed, learn how to recognize your natural way of doing things. Again, we are all products of where we come from.

Your Roots Have Shaped You

Being honest about your roots and how they've shaped you is not always easy. We want to see ourselves as individuals who can do whatever we want with our lives. This feeling may intensify now that you are in the United States, the land of opportunity and choices. The exciting possibility of transformation is one of the joys of traveling and studying abroad —as well as living in general.

My recommendation to international students is this: You know yourself, your life, and your culture. Think about why you are who you are.

I myself grew up in Brazil during a time of tremendous economic volatility. During my teenage years, people were unable to withdraw money from their checking accounts because the government had put a freeze on all withdrawals. You basically could not access your own money. It was a very controversial economic plan at the time. I remember the stress in my family, and the conversations my father would have with my mother about money matters. I remember watching the evening news and hearing politicians trying to explain what they were trying to do. I was about 16 years old at the time. Events like this helped me develop into a conservative individual in my decision making, including career-related choices.

Compare this mindset to that of many Americans, who have historically been bullish about their future, willing to take chances, to innovate, to start businesses, to invest in stocks as opposed to bonds, to comfortably risk failure in search of reward. My upbringing prevented me from developing these characteristics, and the choices I have made professionally reflect this conservatism. Being wrong is a necessary step in problem solving, particularly as problems get more complex. It's hard for me to get back on my feet once I stumble. It wouldn't be wise for me to apply for jobs that would require me to innovate constantly, to accept that failing and experimenting are what lead to great ideas and products. These are key characteristics required for success in many roles. My culture did not prepare me for these types of jobs. My culture has prepared me, however, to live in a constant mode of adaptation. While risk averse, I can "go with the flow" and quickly improvise and essentially be highly adaptive. The economic instability that marked my years in Brazil forced adaptation to the context. While I don't purposely seek change, I am well prepared to deal with it. My past has primed me to be highly adaptive and to also pursue knowledge about a variety of subjects and the world. As is the case with many international students, I have learned to function with limited resources and to appreciate and seize opportunities that have come my way.

What kinds of careers and jobs has your culture prepared you for, or not prepared you for?

Cultural Context As Job-Search Strategy

Predicting an individual's attitudes and preferences toward certain jobs or careers solely based on nationality is imprecise and dangerous, of course. No career coach I have ever met directs students to specific jobs and career paths solely based on nationality. It would be irresponsible to do so. Culture, however, is an important variable that international students must analyze when thinking about what jobs might best fit them. The behaviors your culture has instilled in you might may make you a better fit for certain jobs and career paths than others.

I am not simply suggesting that international students should immediately consider quantitative or science-dependent careers—or STEM careers—which many consider to be more accessible compared to careers that heavily rely on social and communication skills, which may be more challenging for some international students due to linguistic and cultural differences. What I am talking about is something much deeper: it is your potential inability to disagree with your managers when you know they are wrong and the situation calls for you to challenge them. If you come from a culture with a high level of respect for authority, then ignoring hierarchical structures—which is needed at certain times in certain roles—may require a tremendous amount of muscle flexing on your part. This could lead to increased stress and a decrease in job satisfaction and productivity over time. No matter how great your English might be, and how comfortable you may be defending and explaining your position, you may just not be able to get yourself to disagree with your boss. Similarly, if you are an indirect communicator who normally avoids conflict, will you be able to comfortably disagree with a client who complains to you about the price of a consulting engagement they received from your firm? Will you be ready to push back?

Let Your Roots Guide You, Not Limit You

As an international student, you bring to the United States your values, religious beliefs, customs, and assumptions, all of which are products of your societal upbringing and are part of your DNA. We are all products of the environment we grew up in, and that is what is key. You don't get a clean slate when you arrive in the United States as an international student.

You are not a blank canvas when you get off a plane and enter the U.S. as an international student.

Are you the excellent programmer and algorithm whiz kid from India who helped everyone with their computer challenges? Are you the student from China who does not give up until you solve difficult Math problems? U.S. employers are interested in hiring you for what you naturally do well. Start pinpointing country-specific skills and traits that you may have always taken for granted, whatever those might be.

Successful job-search strategies must fit all of an individual's strengths —including strengths rooted in one's home culture. Aligning what you do with who you are culturally can be extremely powerful and satisfying. International students have a unique opportunity to honor and market strengths bestowed by their culture to get hired.

"Our ability to succeed at what we do is powerfully bound with where we are from".

Malcolm Gladwell from *Outliers*

5

Become A Global Networker

Looking for a job is a team sport in the United States, and you'll need to build alliances and relationships with faculty, career advisors, alumni, and even strangers, gaining people's trust so they'll want to help you by referring you to jobs they may hear about, for example. President Obama didn't get elected on his own. He had supporters who coached him, believed in him, cheered him on, opened doors for him, and wanted him to win. Who will be your supporters during your job search in the United States? You'll need them. The best jobs out there often get filled by referrals. The subject of this chapter, networking, is of critical importance. As a job seeker and a newcomer to the United States, you'll find that the job-search process will require you to reach out to people to ask for their help understanding a number of issues, including what career path you may want to pursue, or which companies in your field or industry might be open to sponsoring. International students usually don't have a large base of contacts when they first enter the United States, which means you'll have to develop new relationships in order to increase your chances of uncovering quality job leads.

You can choose to run the job-search marathon alone, without seeking much help or assistance from anyone, but this is a harder path. Why take this path when there are alternative job-search methods that yield better results and maybe even great friendships along the way? Savvy international students understand that it is often through relationships that they can secure a great H-1B job. If you want to discover quality job leads; bypass ineffective ways of applying for jobs, such as submitting resumes online; and maybe overcome sponsorship challenges, then networking is a must. Come graduation time, when the pressure of finding a job usually intensifies, if you haven't invested enough time building a base of contacts in the United States, then you'll be trying to finish the job-search marathon on your own. This is not a good situation to be in. International students who develop a few good connections during their studies—sometimes one or two mentors is all you need—will have help from others, and that can make ALL the difference in the world.

Companies leery of international job applicants may shut doors in your face, but your new contacts in the United States won't. They don't care if you need a visa to work here, and they don't have to become your best friend in order to help you achieve your goals. They need to feel your drive, your sincerity, your hard work, and it's even better if they like you. If people sense you're doing the right things, they may just want to help you.

Getting comfortable networking with strangers is crucial; yet this is very difficult for many international students, who are used to seeking advice only from people they know, such as family members. In the United States, strangers with expertise are more respected than family members in some ways. Some international students are shy, many are worried about their language skills, and many would rather have a root canal than initiate conversation and ask career advice from someone they have never met before. This chapter is meant to help you overcome these worries and make networking fun. You can never network enough, and it's never too early to start. If you've been accepted into a U.S. college—even if you haven't yet left your home country—why not start networking right away? Strangers you meet online, such as through the comments section of a blog or through Linkedin or Facebook can all be part of your job-search journey if you engage with them correctly. You will learn just what to do to connect with people in a genuine way in this chapter.

Worst Fear, Best Chance

Networking can be both productive and fun, and it has been the job-search cornerstone for many international students who found great jobs in the United States. When I ask international students who have secured quality H-1B jobs for their #1 job-search tip, many immediately say "networking." Then I ask, "Do feel you spent as much time networking as you should have when you were in college?" The answer is almost always no. Now that they have started working and find themselves having conversations with their colleagues about how they found their jobs, they often hear the same response over and over: somebody they knew knew somebody, who knew somebody, who then told HR or a hiring manager to take a serious look at their resume. The realization of how critical networking is seems to come later for many international students, once they join the workforce and learn that their colleagues got their jobs through referrals or some sort of connection.

Savvy international students focus on creating genuine, long-term relationships with those they meet throughout their studies in the United States. You don't need to look far. Your professors, your new friends, your neighbors, someone you meet at a cooking class you take on a whim, someone you play volleyball with—all these people can be part of your job-search journey.

When meeting Americans during your studies, you may notice how nostalgic many seem to get when talking about their college years. This is great news for any student, but it is particularly good news for international students who need to create new connections in a new country.

The label "college student" usually gives you a green light to engage with others. "Americans seem very comfortable interacting with college students, even those they don't know. It's almost like they feel it's safe," an international student from India once told me. I agree with this student's very astute observation!

How It Feels

Despite the encouragement to go out and network this is often what I hear: "It feels fake, Marcelo." The idea of connecting with people —sometimes strangers—so they may help your job search seems odd. Worse: it feels dishonest, because you feel like you're using people. And that's the initial problem with networking: it's understood that the only reason you're talking to people at events like business receptions is to advance your job search. The second challenge is that some of us are intensely social, while there's another group of us who are quiet and normally don't get too excited about the business of meeting people.

As if it weren't bad enough to talk to people you don't know, you may feel that it is your job to promote your skills and professional experiences to those you meet. That's going to feel boastful. Approaching someone you don't know to discuss your qualifications will feel as if you're "bragging," which is almost never easy for international students. It's more than just overcoming anxiety and accepting risk: networking is something many international students have never done in their lives. The concept, therefore, is hard to grasp and harder to execute. The word "networking" may not exist in the vocabulary of many languages. Often, the term is borrowed from American English.

Make Networking Fun

So how can you ease your networking anxiety and actually make networking fun? Let's take a look at some strategies.

Share Your Real Story

When you meet people at your school, at a party, or at a business function, talk to them about what it means to be an international student. Let your enthusiasm and fears be known. Tell people why you left China, India, South Korea, or whatever country you're from to come to the United States to pursue a college degree. Share with people your "real" story, not just your professional goals. Consider these questions:

- What was your "real" motivation for wanting to leave your country to go overseas?

- What's your "real" story?

- Why did you choose the United States and not another country?

- What do you think of your experience so far of being an international student?

Communicate with people in an honest way. Start sharing something about your international life and your *true* desire to come to the United States. You didn't come to the United States just to get a diploma from a U.S. university and advance your career. There's probably more to it than that. Feeling comfortable opening up and sharing something truly personal about your international journey allows you to build rapport, and others will want to learn more about you. This goes beyond sharing a hobby—it's deeper and much more personal. It's about your journey.

I was once contacted by a student from Venezuela who wanted some tips on how he could increase his odds of securing an H-1B job. When I asked this student why he decided to come to the United States in the first place, this is what he shared with me:

I could not deal with the uncertain political situation in my country. I came to the United States to keep my dreams alive. I hope somehow to be able to give back to my country, but for now I need to invest in my future.

How do you feel about this student's response? I'll tell you how it made me feel: I was *immediately* drawn to this student. I wanted to learn more about him, and I remember feeling excited about beginning our conversation. Notice that this student did not mention anything about what field of work he was interested in or what jobs he was trying to target.

You can do the same. You can also choose to speak about your hometown and how your culture has shaped you: maybe what you like about your country, what you don't, and what you miss. If you do this naturally, people will start falling in love with you, because your story is refreshing and interesting. It is also a rare story: the story of someone who is brave and not afraid to take chances. You might approach it this way:

I come from a town two hours outside of Beijing, China, where the last Olympic Games took place. This is my first time in the United States—my first time outside my country. It's interesting to be in the United States when there's so much talk about China and how the future of our countries might be linked in different ways. I enjoy listening to the news about the relations between the United States and my country.

As an international student, you are in a perfect position to have great conversations with those you meet about the current state of international relations between your country and the United States.

Here is another example you can use:

I wanted to push myself, see the world a little bit, and pursue a college degree in the United States. I had been studying English for seven years in my hometown in South Korea and felt I was ready for college life in the United States. I get many interesting questions from my friends and family about life in the U.S.

If people like what you tell them, they'll come back for more. People will be naturally curious about your life and the world you come from. They'll want to learn more about you because your story is a little unusual; it's not something they hear all the time. Often, they themselves will ask, "What is it that you want to do?" If they like you, they may open their networks to you. When you reveal something real about your life, your dreams, and your true desire to leave your country to pursue a college degree overseas, you'll notice that you'll connect with people on a completely different level. Students have told me that new acquaintances have said to them, "Wow! I can't imagine going to a foreign country and pursuing a college degree in a language other than my own." One student I worked with told me an alumnus said, "You're so brave. I should encourage my son to consider studying abroad as well." Many people, right off the bat, will give you the credit you deserve as an international student and will want to learn more about your journey. Give people a chance to appreciate and celebrate your international life. Never take your story for granted.

Strive for Real Conversations

What people ultimately want is to have a real conversation with those they interact with. And this, I found, works particularly well in the United States, because it's often what people don't expect. People may assume you'll make quick comments about the weather—"It's a beautiful day, isn't it?" Skip U.S. small talk. Have real conversations with those you meet so you can have some fun and become memorable at the same time.

As human beings, we are wired to want to connect with others, and connecting with someone who is international is cool.

Ready to take your conversations to the next level? Consider this example:

> *I hear much debate about whether or not it is a good thing for the United States to allow international students to remain in the country and work after graduation. Some people feel that international students who stay in the United States may be taking jobs away from U.S. citizens. At a time when the U.S. economy seems slow, this point of view may have some merit. What do think about this issue?*

You're probably feeling a little nervous now; maybe you think I have completely lost my mind. But think about it: it would be a shame if you did not have these types of real conversations with people. When you approach topics with an open mind and a desire to learn rather than to impose your views, almost any conversation is okay. Authenticity inspires respect and a desire to learn more about others.

The general idea is to introduce topics of conversation that draw on your international background and give people a glimpse into your thoughts, opinions, and intelligent worldviews. Talk about the lack of democracy in China and your feelings about it. Talk about the caste system that exists in India and how it may influence who you end up marrying. These are the topics worth talking about. These are the conversations worth having. You have a priceless perspective on all of these issues, so have stimulating, global conversations with people you meet. It would be a shame—a wasted opportunity—if you didn't.

As the world shrinks, boundaries disappear, and the Internet brings everybody together, we can quickly learn about an interesting strategy a company in Uruguay is executing. Old assumptions are quickly challenged or improved upon. What will the future of management look like, for instance? International students studying business, as an example, could easily incorporate this topic into their conversations with new contacts in the United States. You should know by now that you are uniquely positioned to have global, fresh conversations with those you meet.

According to Thomas Hout, adjunct professor at the Fletcher School at Tufts University, and David C. Michael, senior partner and managing director at the Boston Consulting Group, "The future of management lies somewhere between the top-down reform of Western corporations and the bottom-up maturation of Chinese companies." According to the authors, "They have much to learn from each other." These views and other predictions about the future of management appeared in a 2014 *Harvard Business Review* article called "A Chinese Approach to Management." What is your opinion of their views? Whatever it is that you are studying, share with others your own global insights about the field you are interested in. The world is tiny and countries are more than ever borrowing best practices from one another.

Share Your Feelings

When Brazil lost to Germany 7 to 1 at the World Cup, many people from my neighborhood, work colleagues, and friends asked me to make sense of what had happened. Many offered their apologies. My standard reply was this:

> *It was wild what happened. Maybe Brazil will have a new brand going forward. I definitely think something good could come out of this crazy, weird loss.*

When I meet new people these days, I don't hesitate to share my feelings and opinions on a variety of topics. Whether you have an accent or not, you will be memorable when meeting Americans when you share your thoughts and views.

Incorporate Your Background

Take the road less traveled and incorporate elements of your international background into your conversations. Consider this example:

> *I have enjoyed being raised in Italy, where family connections are so strong. While I get homesick sometimes, studying in the United States is a priceless opportunity for me. I'm sure it will transform me in ways I cannot even envision at this point. I'm very grateful for the chance to be attending an American university.*

Family is always an interesting topic of conversation, because it is one that all of us can quickly relate to. Many international students come from collectivist countries where family bonds are strong. Talk about what you think that means, or how this family closeness may make you feel if you stay in the United States after graduation. The idea is to let others get a glimpse of your life, because it is such an interesting life. Your pride in who you are and where you come from will inspire trust.

You can also discuss the similarities and differences between your home country's values and economic system and those in the United States, and draw interesting comparisons. Below is an example I have used dozens of times when people ask me why I came to the United States:

> *You can take classes from different departments as an undergraduate student in the U.S. I find it important to explore different subjects before selecting a major. In my country, you're pretty much*

stuck in your department from day one and often allowed to take classes only there. In fact, you declare your major before getting accepted into college.

You can also briefly explain how higher education in your country differs from the U.S. model. The compare-and-contrast model works well for a variety of topics. It showcases how global you are, and how you "get" life in the United States. Help others learn something new and interesting about you and the country you come from. Notice that you're still not talking about your skills or what kind of job you want to get in the United States.

When networking, always show a sincere interest in the culture of the country you're now living in. Ask for people's views and opinions about their own culture and customs, and ask them to explain facts about life in the United States that may not be very familiar to you. They probably have never taken the time to think too much about these things and will appreciate your questions. Take a look at this example:

People in the United States seem so friendly. Strangers greet one another in supermarkets and so on. When Americans meet one another and ask, "How are you doing?" is this simply a greeting, like saying "Hello," or does the person asking the question really expect the other to answer in detail?

When you meet someone at an alumni function at your school, how about using the following question as a conversation starter:

Thanks for coming to our event tonight. I'm an international student from China. This is my first time in the United States. If you don't mind, let me ask you this question: what do you think is the biggest thing that defines being an American?

You came to the United States to challenge yourself and learn new things, and not to necessarily force yourself to fall in love with sports you may know nothing about, or may not enjoy. You may not be able to cite American football statistics in casual conversation when networking, but you can learn to be comfortable saying:

> *I'm still learning about life in America. American football looks mysterious to me. All is see is people jumping on top of each other. There's nothing quite like it in my country.*

People will appreciate your openness and willingness to learn, and some humor can never hurt. Take a genuine interest in your new country. Strive to improve your cultural fluency in ways that are fun so you can increase your chances of getting hired for roles where "fit" might be an important hiring criterion. Chapter 7, Understanding Fit, will cover what this nebulous concept and key hiring criteria.

Build a Strong Network by Increasing Your Likability

Think about the people you know and like: you like them because you know and trust them. A student once asked me, "Marcelo, am I likeable?" What an excellent question. She understood how critical—and fuzzy—this networking *and* hiring criterion can be, and she had the courage and maturity to ask this question. For certain types of U.S. jobs, much of the hiring seems to be based on "personality" or "likability". This may bother international students who might be used to a more transparent and objective hiring process based on tests scores or GPAs, for example. There is no need to fear likeability: we're all likeable when we feel comfortable sharing something that defines who we are, and that includes our fears and sometimes our flaws. We're all likeable when we show gratitude and when we're willing to learn and ask for advice. Whether you have an accent or not, whether you are an introvert or an extrovert, whether you are westernized or not, people want to know you, the real you.

Implement the suggestions below to increase your likability. Being likeable is key to getting hired and also getting ahead once you secure your job. The opportunity to be likeable is available to anyone who is willing to display the right kinds of behaviors that draw others towards them. You don't need to fall in love with American football to be liked, or speak perfect English either. In fact, your accent and lack of knowledge about life in the U.S can be a great starting point to get others drawn to enjoy you if you are willing to be vulnerable. Below are some behaviors you can display during your studies in the United States that will increase your likability factor.

- **Smile** when you see people you often interact with such as your professors and your career advisors and say, "Good to see you."

- **Compliment** people often. Americans love flattery! Maybe we all do. Say, "That was a great lecture today Professor Johnson."

- **Thank** people. Email your career coach one day and say: "I know that working with international students can be challenging sometimes. You are always patient with me and you really work hard to try to understand my unique job search challenges. Thank you for all you do to help me and my international friends". Similarly, before an interview starts, establish good eye contact with your interviewer and say: "I do appreciate the opportunity to be speaking with you today". At the end of the interview, say, "Thank you for your time. I hope you have a productive day at our school."

- **Ping** people. Let people you know you were thinking of them. Send your career advisor a picture of your hometown and family when you go home during your school break. Say, "This is the house I was raised in in Taipei, Taiwan. Hope you're doing well. I just wanted to say "hello".

Similarly, send an email to your contacts in the U.S. sharing interesting stories about your adventures as an international student. Don't just contact people when you need something from them.

- **Get personal.** Show a sincere interest in whomever it is you are talking to. Ask questions that indicate you are curious about the life If your career coach asks you what kinds of jobs you are targeting, maybe you can ask him or her the following before you answer the question: "Do you mind telling me how you made the career decisions you have made? I'd love to learn more about how you have managed your own career."

- **Nod** your head. When someone is speaking with you nod your head to demonstrate agreement and that you are listening. This helps whoever you are talking to feel connected to you.

Don't try to be someone you are not. Don't implement the suggested techniques I am presenting to you here simply because I encouraged you to do so. You have to believe in what you are doing. Always be genuine. If you did not like Professor Johnson's lecture do not walk up to her and say "That was a great lecture you gave today". But if you did truly enjoy the lecture, sending your professor a short email after class or expressing your gratitude in person if possible is appropriate, so do that!

Your resume, the brand of your school, and your skills will help you secure interviews. But in the end, once you have proven you can get the job done, it is your likability that you will help you get the job. What interviewers will notice and remember about you is whether or not they liked speaking with you. If you take the time to show respect and appreciation towards those you interact with, that can do wonders for you. Displaying the right kind of behavior not only makes you more memorable and likeable but it also makes people want to help you when you need help.

An article titled *Why Likability Matters More at Work*, published by Sue Shellenbarger on the Wall Street Journal in March of 2014, the author cited a study in which researchers at the University of Massachusetts re-viewed the performance of 133 managers and discovered that if an auditor is likable and gives a well-organized argument, managers tend to comply with his suggestions, even if they disagree and the auditor lacks support-ing evidence. Isn't this interesting? Based on this study one can conclude that likeable individuals are more easily able to move their agendas for-ward *even* when they may lack credibility in their recommendations.

I'll take an average but likeable student over a su-per smart but not very likeable student any day as an advisee. Professors and career advisors remem-ber likeable students more easily; even if they are not super stars. They are more inclined to help them succeed and improve. These students are more apt to get hired and at times beat more qualified candi-dates. American employers are not shy about stating that they want to hire people they like.

As a career advisor and mentor to college graduates, the students that standout in my mind as more like-able are the ones who said hello to me, smiled, and thanked me for trying to help them. Then there is a very small group of students who took the time to ask me questions like: "What is it like to help in-ternational students achieve their job search goals Marcelo?" and listened to my answer. This small group of students took a genuine interest in my pas-sion. For this special group I went the extra mile. I launched calls to prospective employers to open doors for them without them knowing. The choice to be likeable is available to all of us.

Share Your Fears and Ask for Help

Psychologist Shalom Schwartz[1] has studied the principles that matter the most to people around the world. In one study, which involved a large sample of respondents from 12 countries, he demonstrated that no matter where people are from, in general, they like to help. In most of the world—including the United States—*giving* is people's most important value, beyond even power and achievement. People like to give more than anything else. Across societies, benevolence—the desire to do good to others—was ranked as number one.

This should be reassuring news to international students looking for jobs in the United States, because you will need help, and people are predisposed to want to help. Americans, in my opinion, will expect you to take the initiative and ask for help when you need it.

You will have to take ownership and responsibility for your success and show a lot of drive and motivation to accomplish your goals. Taking responsibility for your success does not mean you shouldn't seek assistance. In fact, you should do just the opposite. Let others assist you. The more you engage, the more people will want to help you.

When you ask others for help in a genuine way, you are not inconveniencing anyone.

If you think about it, what you're doing is giving people a chance to share with you what they have learned, which is going to make them feel good. In my experience, international students do not reach out

---

[1] Shalom H. Schwartz is a social psychologist, cross-cultural researcher, and author of *Theory of Basic Human Values*, a famous study that investigated what matters the most to people around the world.

enough to engage others who might gladly assist them with their job-search goals. They are not asking for help enough. If your outreach comes from a true desire to learn—as opposed to wanting job leads or access to someone's network—then always reach out.

Still feeling unsure about networking? Well, let others know that's the case. Next time you go to a business reception, look for a friendly face in the crowd, and then offer the following:

> *Hi. Thanks for coming to this event. I am an international student from Japan. May I ask you a question about networking, please? Where I come from, such a concept does not exist. I am confused about what networking is, and what it isn't. How do you approach networking?*

With a statement like this, won't you come across as insecure and unready to function in the United States? Won't your chances of ever finding a job through this individual be diminished if you approach the conversation this way? The answer is no. There is value in honestly revealing your insecurities. Remember: you are not applying for a job. You are trying to develop genuine rapport with someone you've just met.

Brene Brown, a professor at the University of Houston School of Social Work, spent six years trying to understand what separates those who connect easily with others from those who struggle to connect. Brene's research findings taught her that successful connections are available to those who "have the courage to open up, connect with others, and tell the story of who they are with their whole heart." If you come from a country where such open communication is the norm, you won't need to be trained on how to communicate with others this way. The challenge for some international students is believing that it is okay to communicate with others in such a vulnerable way. In a country where the answer to the question "How are you doing?" is almost always "Great," "Pretty good,""Very well," or even "Fantastic," one wonders if there is room for anyone to say, "I am really not doing well at all."

The concept of expressing vulnerability, coupled with the true desire to learn and the courage to ask for help, can make you unstoppable when networking. It does work. Remember: the world of work, jobs, and careers is new for you as an international student. Why not let others know your fears and questions?

Be in Learning Mode

With so many possible majors and careers paths, you may be unsure what to choose, even if you've engaged with your career center. Consider the statement below:

> *I feel my background might be a fit for roles that require creativity and technical work. I have thought of graphic design. There may be other interesting career paths in the United States that I don't know about. Do you have any tips about options I should consider?*

People will respect and like you when you share your insecurities and ask for their advice. In the example above, the student says that she "feels" her background "might" be a fit for roles that require creativity and technical work. What she is really saying is that she's not sure if the career choice she might be making is the best one for her. Essentially she's inviting the person she's talking to assist her in ensuring she is on the right path. She is signaling that she's open and is seeking feedback. By speaking tentatively the student quickly builds rapport. Research shows that this form of communication is more powerful than communicating in a way that projects total confidence and control, which is often what international students feel they need to do when meeting others. International students often do not speak tentatively when networking and often don't ask for enough validation regarding possible career choices to choose from, for example. Learn to speak this way and you will actually gain influence, create stronger connections with those you meet, and more naturally establish rapport and trust.

Take advantage of how little you know about the world of work in your host country as an international student.

You don't need to always appear in control, because you aren't. This is not your country. It's perfectly normal that you are not very sure about how to network, or what possible career paths might suit you. There's much you don't know, and in a way that is great because it allows you to ask those you meet basic but critical questions that could help you better understand what you need to do to achieve your job search goals. The way to achieve success when networking is to be in learning mode at all times. People often respond very well to that. Humility is attractive, and international students tend to be humble. The message around branding, delivering a flawless elevator pitch, and promoting yourself with confidence 24/7 seems to hit international students the minute they get off the plane in the United States. It's natural to feel pressure to always offer value—to sell yourself—to your classmates, new contacts, and even your career advisor. Forget the notion of self-promotion when networking. Ask others for input and advice regarding the unique job-search challenges you'll be facing. You always learn more when you listen, and those you talk to will be more drawn to you if you behave this way.

The Right Balance

International students frequently observe how great American students are at talking about their skills, strengths, and what they want out of life.

"Sure they are," I tell them. "You may never be as good as they are at promoting yourself. But you can still get hired, be a productive worker, and have a fulfilling career." I try to explain to my international students that before going to college, their Americans colleagues have had about fifteen years of practice promoting themselves as part of a culture that highly supports this behavior. American parents often encourage their kids to feel good about their accomplishments, honor them, and speak about them proudly. "Tell Mr. Barros what grade you got on your math test, Jordan," says Jordan's mother, my neighbor, as they both approach me. "I got an A, Mr. Barros," Jordan tells me confidently, with a spark in her eye, a big smile on her face. As a college student, Jordan might be the first one to volunteer to share her elevator pitch during a career-center workshop. American students have a cultural advantage when it comes to selling themselves compared to many international students.

Workshops from career centers focused on "mastering your elevator pitch" or "branding yourself" seem to indicate that this is the ticket to success: being able to tell the world how great you are. The United States is a very sales-driven society. The pressure to "sell"—whether through a LinkedIn request or during a networking event—has distracted international students from developing a simple formula when networking for authentically connecting with those they meet. International students have inadvertently become so focused on "selling themselves" and "showing value" that they've forgotten the simple foundation of effective human interaction: honesty.

When networking and conducting informational interviews, it's perfectly appropriate to speak about past professional experiences and skills you may have developed, but it is critical that you be frank about your hopes and challenges and ask for advice. See the example below:

> *"I feel I have some good math skills, but I am uncertain about what career path to focus on. There are so many majors I don't understand. What do you think I should explore?"*

When you network, the way to impress people is not by selling yourself. Others will naturally be drawn to you and be naturally curious to learn more about you and your professional goals when you first share with them your doubts.

As an international student, you're operating under rules of engagement that have subtleties you don't know much about yet. This is great because it allows you to ask more basic questions, which can help you secure the job you want. So take advantage of these opportunities to learn and grow, and intentionally communicate in a way that projects openness and invites others to want to help you. You already have a reputation for being smart and capable as an international student. You have great skills. You know about computers, you speak two or three languages, you're often great at math, and you're hardworking. But you also have fears, doubts, and questions about the business of meeting people, which can be extremely complex, particularly in a multicultural environment. Share your insecurities, and ask for help. Ask good broad questions. Listen attentively. Advice seeking indirectly allows you to utilize one of the most effective networking strategies in a genuine way: flattery.

Validate your career direction when networking. Below is an example a student from Japan shared with me that she used during a networking event at our school:

> *I have eight years of experience in commercial lending and treasury functions at Sumitomo Bank, both in Japan and in the United Kingdom. After graduation, I think it makes sense for me to leverage my analytical skills to work for a hedge fund that focuses on finding investment opportunities markets in Asia. What other areas do you think someone with my background might want to explore?*

BECOME A GLOBAL NETWORKER

Tell Them You're an International Student

When meeting or writing to a new contact via LinkedIn, consider adapting the following example, which has proven to be effective for many international students:

> *Hello. I'm an international student from South Korea. I have been in the United States for 60 days and don't have many contacts yet who work in your field. Would you mind answering a few questions about your current role? Would you have 15 minutes to speak with me? Thank you very much.*

Your sincerity, honesty, and openness will always go a long way. People can tell, even in an email, if your outreach to them is genuine.

Leave Your Elevator Pitch Behind When Networking

Whenever alumni come to campus to meet with current MBA candidates, I always try to get a sense of how their conversations with international students went. What I often hear is something along the lines of, "The student I talked to seemed to have good strengths, but it seemed like he was really trying to sell himself to me. I never got a chance to get to know him." Next time you go to a networking event, even if someone asks you right off the bat what you plan to do after graduation, take a step back and share a memorable fact about yourself, which might be grounded in your home country. "Thank you for the question," you might say. "Before I answer it, please allow me to quickly tell you what made me want to come to the United States in the first place."

Tricks of the Trade

International students need to know these additional strategies for networking:

1) <u>Establish a network of Americans.</u>

This is often the missing link: sometimes it is the reason international students don't improve their chances of finding a job in the United States. Forming close relationships with Americans continues to be one of the biggest challenges international students face. Use the frameworks in this chapter to help you naturally connect with Americans. What do you like to do for fun? One of the easiest ways to develop connections with Americans is to join interest groups, such as social media meet-ups or a sports club at your school. Enrich your life to have a more well-rounded experience in the United States. Speak with people of different ages and social and academic backgrounds. Talk with a child who is 10 years old and also with someone who is 80 years old and never went to college. A strong base of contacts with Americans increases your chances of creating a team of individuals who want to run the job-search marathon with you and help you along the way. Never use people, of course. Get out there as often you can, meet some great people, and enrich the quality of your experience in the United States. Make a couple of good friends along the way, and find a couple of mentors as well. Your initial motivation for meeting people is to share, learn, help, and have fun. Job leads will come as a result of that.

Say you become friends with an American student who's taking some of the same classes you are. Over Thanksgiving, the American student returns home and tells his parents, "Mom, Dad, I'm friends with this guy from China, who's super smart and wants to get a job in accounting in the United States. Do you know anyone he might be able to talk to?" Sometimes that's all you need. Friends help friends. To build such relationships, you'll need to open up about yourself.

2) Build a network of international students like you.

This is easy, because international students like to help one another. It's nice to get moral support, general cultural tips, and maybe leads of companies and jobs from others who are or were in the same situation you're in.

3) Seek mentors who care about you

If approached correctly, no one will mind answering questions you may have about the job search process. Seek assistance often! Such connections can turn into fulfilling mentorships—and maybe friendships—that can help you navigate everything from job fairs to visa requirements. Once an initial contact is made, maintain a network of contacts who could provide them with job leads during your studies and, perhaps most importantly, who could become lifelong friends. Use the frameworks on this chapter to nurture the relationships with those you meet.

4) Venture beyond familiar territory.

When trying to improve your cultural fit, you won't help yourself if you spend too much time with students from your home country. If you are a graduate student pursing a degree in engineering or computer science, for example, you may look around and feel you are still at home. Some majors have more students from China and India these days than American students. Depending on the degree you're pursuing in the United States, you may have to *intentionally* create opportunities to meet Americans, because it may not happen naturally.

Final Thoughts

International students looking for a job in the United States are about to start playing a contact sport. When playing basketball or soccer, a referee will call a foul. But when you're networking, there will be no referee telling you if you contacted people the "right way" or not. You have to be your own referee. There are specific communication skills you need during networking and informational interviews[2] that differ from those you may utilize when interviewing. If you remember to implement the simple tips below, you'll be fine:

- Be genuine

- State your intentions

- Don't worry about your accent

- Thank people for their time, and respect their time

- Listen attentively

- **Don't ask for a job**

- **Don't sell yourself**

- Validate. *Do you feel I am moving in the right direction? What would you do if you were in my shoes?*

- Show a true interest in the life of the person you're talking to. *If you had to start all over, would you make the same career choices you made?*

- Share your story

- Display utmost professionalism

---

[2] When you arrive in the United States, you'll be encouraged to reach out to professionals whose backgrounds appeal to you to learn how they achieved their career goals. This is called an "informational interview."

- If the conversation feels right, ask for the chance to stay in touch. *Is it okay if I connect with you via LinkedIn? I'd love to try stay in touch.*

- Enjoy the moment

Connect with people often, preferably face to face, because that's usually when great things happen. Don't hide behind your computer. The Internet will not find you a job. Ask to meet someone for coffee for a quick chat before they go to work. A little courage goes a long way. Take the initiative and approach people at job fairs, at your school, and at networking events, and have interesting conversations with them. If the conversation ends up being short and awkward—and it may happen —don't get discouraged. Do it again.

As a homework assignment for this chapter, identify some sort of networking event happening near your school. If possible, try to join events where professionals who work in your field of interest gather. Your professors or your career advisor might be able to refer you to industry associations through which you can meet like-minded people. Common interests bring people together. Individuals you meet at these events might end up being great contacts. Attend one of these sessions, build up a little courage, and talk to people. Use the frameworks provided in this chapter and see what happens.

Don't Sell Yourself

During his 2012 commencement speech to the graduates of the University of the Arts, located in London, England, British author and artist Neil Gaiman (who never went to college himself) had the following to share with students he was talking to:

"The moment that you feel that, just possibly, you're walking down the street naked, exposing too much of your heart and your mind and what exists on the inside, showing too much of yourself," he warned — "that's the moment you may be starting to get it right."

Who are you? As an international person you are probably so interesting, but if I don't know your journey, your dreams, your opinions and your failures; if I don't know what you care and don't care about; if I don't know your motivations and insecurities—then I am probably not going to be engaged. Don't tell me you are crazy smart with computers or someone who wants to go into brand management. I have heard all of that before. I want to get to know you. What is your unique voice? Reveal with courage who is behind the different face and accent in the middle of the crowd.

"What we are communicates far more eloquently than anything we say or do."

Stephen Covey from *The Seven Habits of Highly Effective People*

6

SHARING YOUR STORY

The previous chapter, "Networking," examined how international students can create strong and genuine connections with those they meet in the United States by letting their guard down and sharing their dreams and fears, and by asking for advice and help. This chapter, "Sharing Your Story," revisits some of the concepts previously covered, but with a tighter focus on how they relate to interviewing. The discussion about interviewing continues again in Chapter 10, where we will learn from Fang Wang's success.

A hiring manager from Citigroup recently told me over lunch, "I'm not going to hire a student who's not able to tell me a good story." What a great opportunity for international students, I thought. But why is it so hard for international students to share stories that reflect the full range of their professional achievements and capabilities? This chapter will help you maximize the value and impact of your stories as an international student.

Stories Have Purpose

Although passion and authenticity certainly matter when interviewing, you won't be quite as carefree as you might be during networking and in casual conversation. In an interview, you must use your stories and answers to clearly communicate the following:

- You understand the job responsibilities of the position you're applying for, preferably beyond what is written in the job description. You know what you are getting yourself into. You know the good and the bad that comes with the job you want.

- You have the skills, experience, and motivation to be successful in the role.

- The company you're applying to is the right place for you, as opposed to one of its competitors hiring for an identical role.

Those you interview with will always be thinking: do I understand where you've been and where you now want to go?

In other words, how does your previous, pre-U.S. work and life connect to what you want to do professionally after you obtain your degree? The recruiter may have seen your resume and may have spent five seconds glancing over it. But now he or she wants to know what you're all about. Based on what you tell those you meet, and how you tell your story, these individuals will be deciding if you have the ability to reach your professional destination, and how long it will take you to get there.

Connecting the Dots

When meeting with American recruiters and hiring managers, you will have to connect the dots—you'll have to make things very clear—and create the *right linkage* between your pre-U.S. experiences (professional and or/academic) and the new professional chapter you want to add to your life in the United States after graduation. Don't make Americans work to see the connection. Spell it out for them through an impactful and easy-to-follow narrative.

> *I chose that role because…*
>
> *I believe my previous background fits nicely with what I want to do after graduation because…*

Similarly, share insights about previous experiences that are relevant to those you're talking to.

> *As a first job out of school my role as marketing manager validated my desire to do creative work that incorporated analytics.*

Make things clear!

Beyond Tasks

Doubt about the value of pre-U.S. experiences sometimes keeps international students from sharing what they did at home with pride and impact. In general, what most international students are thinking when speaking about their pre-U.S. work or academic experiences is: does anybody really care?

Because of this common doubt, international students often rush through their stories, providing only a "task description" of what was accomplished. They may say, "My job was to create the user interface for the new phone application my firm developed." They don't elaborate on what was needed to accomplish the task (leadership, communication skills, technical skills, etc.), what they learned along the way, and why they may have enjoyed and thrived in the work. American recruiters and hiring managers are looking to learn about all of that.

Make Them Care

During the question and answer (Q&A) part of a presentation by a speaker reviewing job-search strategies for international students, a student from India asked, "How can we convince employers of the unique value that international students may bring to their organizations?" The speaker answered without batting an eyelid, "American employers don't care."

The speaker is correct! Employers won't care until you make them care. It is your job to leverage impactful storytelling that does justice to your pre-U.S. accomplishments and any cultural strengths or traits that your future U.S. employer should know about. International students have a unique opportunity to use powerful storytelling that swiftly incorporates competitive cultural advantages, differentiating them from other candidates. The idea is to signal to employers that there's an interesting dimension to you—the fact that you're international—that translates into real value to them. American employers will not immediately see this connection.

Your first task is to honor the skills, talents, and professional and academic achievements you developed *prior* to coming to the United States. Help those you are talking to visualize "you in action," getting the job done. This is not easy to do, but with practice you can get really good at it. If you don't have work experience, speak about volunteer experiences, or perhaps about a project at school that you really cared about. All these experiences are indicative of your interests, passions, and professional potential.

If you yourself don't understand the value you generated for your previous employers, potential new employers probably won't either. Engage with your career advisor to start solidifying your narrative.

Not Just the Facts

You weren't magically transported to the United States. If you scored high on your GMAT or SAT exam, you did not just get lucky the day of the test. A lifetime of learning prepared you for that moment. You didn't develop exceptional math skills overnight. Due to linguistic and cultural reasons, sometimes international students are not very good storytellers. Culture often gets in the way, rendering it difficult to share successes like making a valuable contribution at work or graduating from a top university back home. Facts aren't enough: you must weave them into a captivating story that puts the correct amount of emphasis on sought-after skills and unique talents that sometimes only you may have.

So how can you turn a high GMAT or SAT score or strong academic performance into a story that gets you hired? If you have the stamina, intelligence, and adaptability to earn a college degree in a foreign country, and sometimes perform better academically than domestic students, you've already revealed a lot about yourself—and how capable a worker you might be. You could get hired *if* you connect the dots for your future U.S. employer the right way.

Recruiters often say that they want to know what a candidate is all about,. An interview is essentially your chance to tell the interviewer your story. Create powerful stories that do justice to the strengths and unique qualities you have developed throughout your life, before you became an international student.

A Point of Reference

Provide a point of reference to help people understand and appreciate your home-country experiences and achievements. For example, if you mention the size of the company you worked for at home, it won't have much meaning unless you can compare it to similar organizations that operate in the United States. Don't let your stories suffer from a lack of context. If your goal is to convince the recruiter that you worked for an organization that generated the most revenue in its vertical, saying only that your employer generated $1 billion in sales doesn't explain how your company compares to others. If it's appropriate, mention that your past employer is a leading provider of [product] and/or a sought-after name among college hires in your country. If you don't include these details, the recruiter or hiring manager won't be able to give you full credit for your achievements.

Providing a point of reference is critical. It's not bragging. You are just trying to help someone understand what you've done. Depending on your background and experiences, you might adapt one of these examples to give recruiters and hiring managers a sense of your achievements:

- I worked for a marketing firm with global clients: P&G and J&J were also customers.

- I attended one of the top five universities in China.

- I worked for the largest energy company in Brazil

- I joined the most sought-after employer for engineering graduates in my country.

Cultural Context

Just as it can be hard for international students to grasp many facets of U.S. society and the world of work, most U.S interviewers and others you talk to will not have knowledge of the industries, work functions, and school system of your country. It is your job, not theirs, to help them understand the particular dynamics of your professional and educational history. Correctly communicate the value of such experiences to your audience so they can understand and appreciate what you've done and give you the credit you deserve.

The most renowned university in Brazil at the time this book was published is a public institution that enjoys some international recognition. Universidade de Sao Paulo has acceptance rates similar to some Ivy League schools in the U.S for certain departments. A U.S. recruiter only used to the dynamics of higher education in the U.S. may find it puzzling that a public university could be ranked higher than any other private school. Here's another example: high school students in certain countries are often focused on passing highly competitive national entrance college exams, and often neglect high school grades in order to focus on what matters the most. High school grades were a useless hiring criteria at the time I left Brazil to come to the U.S, but knowing which university someone got accepted into was key when evaluating recent college hires. Japan has a similar culture: GPAs from Japanese college students are virtually useless when analyzing the potential of recent college hires, but knowing which college a Japanese student attended definitely is not.

Consider this example from a student:

> *I majored in economics. I worked very hard in high school and obtained my degree from a top university in South Korea. After school, I worked for five years as an auditor for a large national bank, equivalent in size to UBS here in the United States, I'd say. I spent most of my time doing traditional financial analysis and internal auditing. I enjoyed my work a great deal. Since starting my MBA, I've been drawn to consulting because it allows me to fully leverage my pre-MBA skill set.*

This student understands the importance of cultural context translation. He found a quick and effective way to "translate" his experience in South Korea to the U.S. context. The fact that his bank was a major player in the financial services industry in his home country needed to be high-lighted, hence the comparison to UBS. Without this comparison, his story would have been flat, and his background would have remained somewhat vague. This student also stated that he attended a top univer-sity in his home country. This is going to feel like bragging for many international students, and it won't be easy. However, if you don't state this fact, nobody will understand the quality of your school.

Delivery

Something else to pay great attention to is *how* you deliver your story. Content *and* delivery are important! What does it mean to be a strong communicator within the context of the United States? It means that your communication is precise, simple, and clear. Your message should not be implied or subtle, because that could cause confusion; Americans will be looking for clarity. Your job is to make your point clear to the listener, without coming across as arrogant. Communication styles vary from culture to culture. Draw the conclusion for the listener. In the pre-vious example, when the student from South Korea says, "I spent most of my time doing traditional financial analysis and internal auditing," he quickly explains what he did. He does not leave the interviewer guessing. Communicate with both confidence and humility, and provide specific examples that back up your claims. That's how your message will register best with Americans.

Strategies to Use

International students have a unique opportunity to become memorable and connect with others by sharing stories about their lives that are fresh and global, stories that recruiters don't often hear and that domestic students are often not able to share. Apply the following suggestions to create powerful stories that get you noticed:

1) Connect with whomever you are talking to.

Be proud of what you accomplished before becoming an international student. Overcome cultural barriers and speak confidently about your successes. Look people in the eye when delivering your stories, and remember how far in life you've come.

2) Use numbers as a point of reference.

Data is important but often needs to be correctly "translated" to fit the U.S. context. Figures add a sense of proportion to your accomplishments and show you understand the impact of your efforts. American employers love this! If you saved your company $10K in long-distance phone charges by recommending the purchase of a new telephone system, this initial number sounds pretty impressive. But were the $10K in savings the largest savings your firm ever realized through a technology purchase, or were the savings not that significant after all? What can you do to put the $10K figure in the best context possible to help others appreciate its real magnitude?

3) Remember that we are all human.

Great stories contain enthusiasm and highlight your learning orientation and even your sense of gratitude. Say "It was a great opportunity to be part of the team that looked at the best ways to merge the databases our firm ended up with after we acquired three new companies." Of course, you can continue to enhance your story by demonstrating what you learned: "We were not initially clear on the best way to merge the databases. Strong brainstorming taught me to consider all possible options before moving too quickly with a solution that was right but not optimal."

4) Great storytelling showcases what you are capable of.

What problem did *you* solve? What was *your* contribution? U.S. employers will want to know what it is that *you* did. Embrace how intelligent you are—a trait international students are known for—and translate it into value for the firm you want to join. To continue with the previous example: "I volunteered to create test scenarios, which included three different possible ways to merge the data, before we moved forward with a final decision. My team approved of the test scenarios I suggested. I ran some tests and shared the results with other members of the task force."

Even if recruiters don't directly ask you the question, they will be interested in knowing the *individual* contributions you made during a group project. The right balance of "we" and "I" is crucial. This may take practice, as many international students are from places where accomplishments are presented as part of a group activity, and often they find it odd /unnatural/boastful to draw attention to their specific contributions to a project.

5) Be expressive.

This can be hard for some international students due to cultural reasons, but it is key from a delivery standpoint. U.S. employers will be looking for hires who are expressive and come across as "open." If you do a good job with the previous recommendations, then you will have automatically addressed tip number #5.

6) Global stories.

International students have a unique chance to share stories that are global in nature. Embrace your global awareness. The goal is to swiftly differentiate yourself and to tell an employer, "I'm ready to excel in the role I'm interviewing for today, but I also have unique characteristics that prepare me to be a successful global manager for your firm in the future."

Paint a picture of long-term possibilities with your future employer that tie into unique traits you have that other candidates don't.

When meeting with global organizations that may do a lot of business with your country or region of origin, you'll need to emphasize why your international background could be an asset. Again, do not assume your interviewers will see this connection. Position yourself as a candidate who has the know-how, global mobility, and technical skills to help a company both short-term and long-term. More and more firms depend on international revenue in order to grow. Help your future employer visualize your growth trajectory inside the firm, which could include an assignment overseas. The more appealing you make yourself to a company by positioning yourself as a candidate that can address *both* their short-term and long-term needs, the better.

7) You fit, but you're also different.

The secret is to deliver a blended message to U.S. hiring managers and recruiters. Market your background creatively by showing how valuable your unique international perspective might be for the role you're seeking. Project a sense that you're comfortable with life in America so your interviewers feel you fit. Chapter 7 will explain exactly what "fit" means.

8) Practice.

Storytelling for international students requires special consideration, but none of the recommendations listed here are difficult to master. With enough practice, you can get really good at telling great stories no matter how you feel about your language skills. You can prepare several different types of stories ahead of your interviews. Your career advisor will be able to help you craft and deliver stories that have great impact by utilizing the traditional "STAR" storytelling methodology (see Chapter 10, "Interviewing") or my preferred "STARE" method, my modified version of the STAR method, which I recommend to international students.

Last but not least, from a delivery standpoint, your stories should be conversational, not memorized. A good interview ends up being a good conversation. Chapter 9, "Communication Skills," and Chapter 10, "Interviewing," will provide more recommendations you can utilize to increase the impact of your stories.

7

PROVING YOU FIT PLUS MORE

Let's imagine you find a job you really like. You review the job requirements carefully, and it seems that whoever wrote them had you in mind. In a previous role, you performed the same exact function in a very similar work environment. You not only liked what you did, but you excelled at it. Everything looks great, so you decide to go ahead and apply for the job. As expected, you get a call for an interview. You have a couple of interviews, and the company confirms that they do sponsor. That's great. Without sponsorship to worry about, you can calmly focus on the interview process. You feel really good about your chances of securing this role. After all, you're clearly a match for the job. Who else could have experience and credentials that align so closely to what the employer is looking for?

You make it to the final round. The employer has displayed all the right "buying signals." They seem genuinely interested in you. A couple of weeks go by, and you don't hear back. You check in with the recruiter by email, but you don't get a reply. You email the hiring manager you interviewed with, and the same thing happens: no response. At this point, you start to worry. The next day, you call the recruiter again. You get lucky, and the recruiter actually answers the phone. You ask for an update on the hiring process. The recruiter says, "I'm sorry I didn't call you back. We've been very busy. We've moved forward with another candidate. We appreciate your interest and wish you the best going forward."

You can barely believe what you've heard. What happened? Did the company find someone that was *more qualified* than you? Maybe, but maybe not. You will probably never know. It's safe to say that whichever candidate the company chose was perceived to be a better "fit" for the job than you were. You feel discouraged, somewhat betrayed, and confused. You thought you understood what the employer was looking for, but maybe you missed something. But what?

Hiring Decisions Are Emotional, Unfortunately

Hiring decisions seem to be emotional, and, in many instances, subjective. The process of deciding who gets hired can be subtle and complicated, and it's sometimes not well understood. Over the years, I have had a chance to ask several hiring managers and HR recruiters from different industries how they know if they're sitting in front of the right candidate. This is what I often hear: "I just know. When I see it, I can feel it." But what does that really mean? The ambiguity around hiring decisions bothers many international students, who might be used to a more transparent, well-defined set of hiring criteria understood by all involved. The emphasis on "fit" confuses international students. In a world driven by analytics, formulas, and algorithms, you would think that someone out there would have developed a scientific way to determine who is the "best" candidate for a given role. Very few companies in my experience seem to rely on data to make hiring decisions.

Many international students believe that their technical skills, knowledge, and grades should be considered above everything else. For certain STEM roles that are highly specialized, that might be the case. If you want to be a programmer and you can prove that you can create a bug-free mobile phone app in two days because of your awesome Java-Script programming skills, you may get hired based on your competency to perform a specific task. But for many jobs out there, the hiring criteria are nebulous at best, and you hear the word "fit" thrown around all the time.

The Role of Grades

Let me make a quick comment about grades before we circle back to "fit." To international students used to working very hard to achieve the highest possible level of academic success, the relaxed expectations that some U.S. recruiters and hiring managers may have about academic performance can be confusing. Some international students come from environments with a non-negotiable focus on education and have always worked incredibly hard, often under intense pressure, to maintain a superior level of academic achievement. It might be disappointing—or a relief—to hear that American recruiters, in general, do not pay much attention to grades or GPAs compared to other hiring factors. For any job you're interested in, find out what the expectations are regarding academic performance. You may learn that you don't have to be one of the best students in your class, and that a 3.5 GPA is more than enough to make you a competitive candidate. Find out what's expected and allocate your time accordingly. If you excel academically, as it is the case with many international students I have met over the years, be proud of your academic achievements, speak about them confidently. Create story telling that highlights how your strong academic performance can translate into value to your prospective employers. Your good grades can be good indicators of abilities you may have. Many jobs out there require math, computer skills, coding, and focus to creatively and critically analyze information and data. If your good grades reflect skills in these areas, you have an advantage.

A Word on Soft Skills

Some international students may fare better when applying for jobs where employers are measuring specific proficiencies rather than cultural fit and soft skills. However, American recruiters and hiring managers often tell career-center professionals that they tend to notice soft skills first—before they can evaluate any hard skills you may have. I'll explain what soft skills are a little bit later. Even when international students come to the United States with proven technical and quantitative expertise, they often don't get the credit they deserve unless they can showcase an adequate level of soft skills, which give American employers some assurance they will be able to function in the role with ease. In other words: that they will fit.

Proving You Fit

If you have successfully advanced to the final stages of an interview process, particularly for high-profile jobs in large firms that are often targeted by college graduates, you have already convinced your interviewers that you possess the skills for the job. As a finalist, now is the time to get people to fall in love with you and to show employers that they'll get more by hiring you because you're an international student.

Fitting in is exactly what many American employers are looking for, and sometimes it's what separates those who get hired from those who don't. "Why didn't I get the job?" many international students have asked me over the years. You may never be able to truly learn why you were not selected, especially when it seems you did everything right. What follows are some unspoken requirements that American employers look for in great hires, and that sometimes international students overlook during the job-search process.

Passion

As discussed in Chapter 3, U.S. hiring managers want more than your abilities; they want your passion, too. The interviewer is looking for assurance that you love what you do: if you do, you'll work harder, but you won't mind because it won't feel like work to you. What evidence can you share that demonstrates your commitment to the industry and the role? Did you keep a blog when you were in school about a topic you are passionate about? Did you offer to help one of your professors with his or her research because you just love the topic and want to learn more about it? Are you an active participant of a relevant industry association? Can you generate your own opinions and insights about whatever it is you love: computer science, engineering, accounting, sports, coffee? If you want to have an impact and attract the attention of hiring managers and recruiters, you have to do something to get noticed and send the world a clear message about your commitment for whatever field you are interested in. A candidate who meets the position requirements and has passion will beat a candidate who meets the requirements but is simply interviewing for a job. Candidates with great passion but weaker qualifications sometimes beat stronger, more experienced candidates. People want to give those who have passion a chance.

Likeability

You spent years in school acquiring knowledge. You've had internships to put into use what you learned. Now, after all this work, you learn that hiring decisions are based on "likeability"? In a nutshell, those interviewing you will be wondering: can I laugh with this person? Will I want to go to lunch with this person? Will this individual be a nice addition to our team? Will our clients like this person? If my boss asks me to share an office with this individual, how will I feel? In other words: do I like this person? If people don't like you, you won't fit. The best way to deal with likeability as a hiring factor is to be yourself. If you're a quiet person, don't try to be an extrovert when interviewing. But remember this: U.S. employers will be looking for candidates who seem open and with whom they can easily interact.

Cultural Fit

No matter how passionate or likeable you are, you won't get hired if you don't fit in with the team you're trying to join, the overall vibe of the company you want to work for, and maybe even the style of your direct supervisor. Ask insightful questions during the interview that demonstrate that you understand how critical all of these issues are. Pay special attention to the style of your future manager. Is the individual low-key or more of a show-off? Is he or she soft-spoken, a listener, or talkative and assertive? You may ask your future manager to describe his or her leadership style. These questions signal that you understand the importance of fit and that you want to ensure that the firm is the right one for you. It's a two-way street at the end of an interview process for highly competitive roles. Once you identify that there is good cultural fit between you, the team, and the firm you want to join, don't be shy, and state what you think: "Based on the information I have gathered, I believe I would be productive and happy in this role. I welcome the chance to join your team."

See the Big Picture

In order to truly ace the interview and get hired, you need to see beyond the job itself. What's the firm trying to do?

International students can often draw on specific aspects of their background that matter to firms they want to work for.

Is the company growing internationally? Do they do business with your home region? How do they approach innovation? Establish a greater vision for the role you are seeking by showcasing the skills and traits you have as an international hire that your manager could utilize in creative ways. This is your opportunity to differentiate.

Be a Good Corporate Citizen

Show your future employer that you can make the company better by being a great corporate citizen and contributing ideas and solutions that only you can offer. Similarly, show interviewers that you care about those you'll work with, that you value them as professionals, that you want to increase the overall performance of the team you want to join by sprinkling in your international personality and insights. You may say, "As an international employee, I would strive to maintain your firm's strong culture and look for ways to make it even better by providing insights that are global."

Look Beyond Job Descriptions

Don't be naïve: job descriptions are very helpful, but rarely do they give you a true sense of what a job is all about. Anything that provides additional insight into your target role gives you an edge during the job-search process. Talk to people who have similar roles to understand what their jobs are truly all about. Get deep knowledge about the industry. If you can identify an employer's true pain points and figure out the unspoken things your future manager really cares about, then you'll be in a good position to craft responses and questions and generate interview strategies that get to the heart of the key issues and show you fit. You can take this idea one step further by positioning yourself as a candidate who will give more than what the employer was hoping to find in a new hire. Your international background often allows you to close this gap.

Embrace the American Entrepreneurial Spirit

No matter what kind of role you seek, U.S. employers will be looking for evidence that you take action when you see an opportunity to make something better or more efficient. Showcase how resourceful you are. Many international students have worked with limited resources before coming to the U.S. and yet their drive and initiative allowed them to achieve great heights.

Soft Skills

Some jobs may require strong soft skills, and these are highly cultural and often very rooted in language fluency. Soft skills usually encompass the following:

- Your ability to work with people

- Your conflict-resolution abilities

- Your presentation skills

- Your ability to communicate well

- Your skill in getting along with clients and gaining their trust

- Your ability to disagree with your client the "right way"

- Your ability to generate more business for the firm

As you can see, soft skills are of great importance. Many international students don't advance in interviews because they may be perceived as candidates who lack the soft skills needed to succeed; as a result, they're sometimes labeled as candidates who don't fit. You've had years to develop strong soft skills in your country. Don't expect to develop strong U.S.-based soft skills overnight. You won't. Soft skills are measured by cultural standards, and you are now operating outside of your culture. In your home country, when you were speaking your own language and were fully in control of your interactions with others, perhaps you were perceived as someone with strong soft skills who could quickly fit and perform well in a variety of situations. Don't expect a typical U.S. hiring manager to be inclusive of linguistic and cultural differences. Spend time socializing with Americans to understand how they behave and think. International students who are willing to push themselves out of their comfort zones tend to develop strong soft skills faster than international students who choose the comfort of their own culture and language. Gaining the soft skills you need to succeed in U.S. jobs where "fit" is important does not need to be an intimidating process for international students, but effort is required. Get out there and have fun.

There's No "I" in "Team"

If you develop a sharp eye for life in the United States, you'll see that successful people engage others to review their work even when they feel 100% certain that what they did is right. American work culture highly values collaboration and teamwork. Many international students are more comfortable working independently and sometimes view team-work as unnecessary and/or unproductive. Make the effort to broaden your thinking.

Let's look at an example. Say you conducted a financial analysis and think you did a great job. Because you've observed how people work in the United States, you decide to invite others to review your work. As a savvy international student, you set up a conference call with various team members from your class—maybe you buy people lunch if you're meeting with them face to face—and present your findings for feedback. You ask people: what do you think of what I did?

Doing great financial analysis may not be the hard part for international students—remembering to engage others to provide input may be more challenging. Remind yourself to partner with those around you to get their perspectives on what you're working on. A fresh pair of eyes might help you improve your work even more.

Strong teamwork skills will be very important for many U.S. roles. People don't work in a vacuum in the United States, and recruiters and hiring managers will be looking for evidence that you can function well in teams. Get used to working in groups and engaging others to review your work often, even when you think it's not necessary. You will learn a lot when you start behaving this way.

Make Your Resume Fit

Even if you haven't worked in the United States, there are things you can do to help your resume fit American expectations. Get a part-time job if possible during your studies, or volunteer somewhere. (Always check with your university before you accept any type of employment or volunteer assignment.) There are several benefits associated with acquiring

U.S. work or volunteer experience. One of them is the chance to observe Americans at work and get a feel for how those who are successful and well-liked behave. Being able to emphasize your engagement with U.S. life, including volunteering and other projects outside of school, might catch the attention of some recruiters. These activities function like a secret message, conveying to a recruiter that you know how to effectively operate in the United States—a positive sign that you'll fit into the workplace culture.

Standing Out

Often, the trick to succeeding as an international student is finding job opportunities where you don't have to try so hard to fit. The following blog post from an MBA student from China who is interested in fashion shows that she understands the idea of fitting in, or not fitting in at all:

Fitting In or Standing Out? Breaking into Fashion, in China Context, by Yang Zhao (This is the real student name. It was not modified)

December 23, 2013

Most international students have some sort of identity crisis when they come to the United States. We are shy; we have accents; we don't get drunk or high too much. Despite the high inclusivity of American culture, we sometimes still feel isolated. So "fitting-in" has become a major part of our social homework.

We talk English to our fellow countrymen; we eat Five Guys and watch football, forcing ourselves to fall in love with a sport we don't even understand. Unfortunately, we still couldn't fit in. We see our more than two decades of foreign lives as "baggage."

Wait a minute. Why fit in when you can stand out? Why not stay special?

This was the new wisdom I found when I was put onto a student panel of a luxury-industry seminar in New York. When it comes to China's luxury market, we are hot! Americans want to pick our brains and know everything we intake and expel. The audience, luxury retailers, exchanged business cards with Chinese on one side, and we added contacts on WeChat. Some rather effortless insights of mine led the way to a casual business lunch with a luxury retail company and another upcoming networking event with some rather prominent business people with China connections. Unfortunately, I cannot disclose any further details until I secure some real opportunities.

Make sure to fully use your regional advantage. Our value is not in how "fitting" we have become in American culture. What makes us special makes us stand out. Find places that look for talent with your specialties and feel proud of them.

8

SOCIAL SAVVINESS

You learned in Chapter 5, "Networking," that the business of getting a job in the United States is personal, and that networking can help you get away from the standard "we don't sponsor" reply that many international students hear when looking for a job.

Your job search will require a great deal of contact with different types of people, and these interactions may bring many cultural differences to light. You'll need social savviness to conduct a successful job search that gets people excited about helping you. You don't have to Americanize yourself to succeed, but you have to be 100% aware of what is happening around you. Your job-search success will be tied to how well you interact with others, virtually and face to face. If you wish to remain in the United States after graduation and build a successful, long-term career here, the importance of developing social savviness cannot be overemphasized.

Good social skills can be learned, and they are worth learning because they may help you convince a recruiter to go up the chain to ask his or her superiors to provide an exception to the current hiring policy so they'll consider interviewing you as an international student. If you are socially adept, you might be able to open doors that might otherwise have been closed. You'll be rewarded when you're socially savvy. You'll often be liked. People will think you're competent, and you may get hired. Good things happen to those who are competent, but great things seem to happen to those who are competent and socially savvy. Aspire to be a charming international student.

Improving Social Savviness

International students are known for being smart. Due to cultural differences, there may be a perception that international students may not have strong social skills, and that can be a problem when you're looking for a job in the United States.

There are two critical strategies for improving your social savviness:

1) Be intensely curious.

Develop an ongoing curiosity about even the simplest day-to-day situations you encounter in the U.S. Observe how people greet one another, and how they complement and disagree with one another. Observe the small talk that takes place every morning at Starbucks.

2) Don't be judgmental.

Make an effort to interpret situations from the perspective of the country's citizens. As an international student, you should appreciate different cultures and perspectives, and be comfortable dealing with people with different views.

U.S. Work Experience As Evidence of Social Savviness

A recruiter from a top U.S. consulting company once indicated to me that while they are open to interviewing international students, they give stronger consideration to international candidates with U.S. work experience.

What this *really* means is that this particular firm is looking for hires who understand core social competencies—social savviness—as Americans. The company wants someone with the ability to create strong relationships with Americans and who understands the dynamics of the U.S. workplace and U.S. life in general. Depending on the types of jobs you're targeting, you may need to demonstrate the same.

American Students' Cultural Advantage

During a trip to China, I approached an alumnus from Shanghai who decided to return home after graduation and asked if I could record his views and tips on how international students could have a successful job search during their studies in the United States. The alumnus became visibly nervous and politely declined to be videoed. When I asked him why, he said, "What if I'm wrong? What if my views and ideas aren't accurate? I don't feel comfortable suggesting to students what they should do. I don't know this field enough." U.S. students, meanwhile, may have jumped at the chance to "build brand" and get more exposure, never questioning whether their advice was sound.

A Common Obstacle

Take a minute to answer yes or no to the following questions. In your opinion:

1. Are you too shy by American standards?

2. Do Americans think you don't contribute enough to team discussions during group projects and homework assignments?

3. Do you think you might be perceived as insecure?

4. Are you afraid of requesting an informational interview from a stranger?

5. Do you spend most of your free time with other international students?

6. Do you dislike the idea of meeting with people face to face?

If you answered "yes" to more than three of these questions, then this is an unscientific signal that you may need to change. There is little reward in the United States for remaining too quiet, particularly when job searching. You have to go after the job you want and deserve—it probably won't just come to you. And in order to do so, your voice must be heard, literally. America was built on the premise that individuals should speak their minds, express how they feel and what they think, and ask for what they believe they deserve. Those who are reluctant to do so may encounter difficulties having their talents acknowledged, even if they are capable. Being too introspective can be dangerous, and it can cost you jobs and opportunities to network and make friends.

People can "hear" silence in the U.S, and sometimes they don't know what to do with it. They may draw wrong conclusions about you, such as that you don't have good social skills. If you're too quiet, people may think you're not passionate or maybe even not smart. During interviews, U.S. hiring managers and recruiters will be thinking: does this individual have the right set of social skills to quickly create trust and strong relationships with others, both inside and outside the firm?

The founding fathers of the United States argued and expressed their ideas with passion and conviction. They made their voices heard and were not afraid of being wrong. Not much has changed: U.S. culture continues to value open dialogue, as well as speed, action, and even healthy conflict, and not always accuracy.

Be Adventurous Every Day

Each one of us has a comfort zone. It's easy and sometimes unproductive to do only what comes naturally. If you know it is easy for you to remain quiet, not engage with others, and simply get behind your computer and start applying for jobs, then monitor this tendency and put a plan in place to help you behave differently.

Here's something you can do: challenge yourself to be a bit adventurous each day. You'll be surprised at how much you can accomplish, how much others will appreciate your outreach, and how fast your social skills will improve. Schedule a meeting with a professor who has studied or taught in your home country to hear what he or she thought of the experience. Meet with a new career advisor to get additional tips about your job search. Say hello to a stranger on a bus and attempt to strike up a conversation. Always be genuine when you have these interactions. If it's tough for you to engage with others, treat it as a game, and you will see how reaching out to others will eventually become second nature. Many people say that they feel like a different person when speaking a language other than their own. This feeling should allow you to take some risks and get out of your comfort zone. Give it a try.

An Inspiring Story

The following story, from an international MS accounting student from China who secured a great H-1B with PwC, may inspire you:

When Li Na, an international student pursuing an MS in accounting, went to an on-campus job fair, she built up the courage to approach a company she liked and asked them if they needed any help with accounting work. The woman she talked to responded, "We're only looking for help with IT work at this point, but I'm happy to keep your contact info, just in case." Li Na responded, "I appreciate that. Thank you so much. I'm hoping to put my accounting skills to use." Li Na wished the woman a nice day and left.

About 45 days later, Li Na received an email that said, Hello, Li Na. We met at your university career fair. Actually, we do need help with accounting work. Are you able to stop by for a chat?

Li Na responded to the email and arranged an interview time—and eventually got hired. She excelled in her role and often thanked her supervisor for the great opportunity she had been given. She also mentioned to her boss that she welcomed help identifying professionals in the accounting industry she might be able to talk to in order to learn from them.

Li Na was in luck. Her boss knew someone at PwC and arranged for her to contact this individual. What started as a casual informational interview turned into a formal interview process, and Li NA eventually became a full-time employee at PwC. Is Li Na smarter than other accounting students in her class? It's tough to say, and it's not that relevant. What is relevant is that she got a great job in the United States, and she did so by being more discoverable. She took more chances. She was not afraid to approach others in a very polite and professional way and ask them if she could assist them with their accounting needs. What separates Li Na from other international students is that she had the courage to engage with someone and offer help.

I had a chance to hear Li Na share her job-search success story at a panel. Other international students listened attentively to her advice. Having lived in the United States for almost two years, she had achieved what so many dream of. After Li Na finished answering students' questions, I approached her myself to see if I could ask her a few more questions about her journey in the United States and her job-search success. As we chatted, it quickly became obvious what kind of impression Li Na must have made when she approached the woman at the college fair who would later become her manager. Li Na did not speak perfect English, but she was not self-conscious about it. She was polite, professional and open, and even thanked me for wanting to speak with her. She made me feel good!

Li Na had this to say about how she developed strong social skills: "I just try to be myself. I try to be polite and sincere, and I try to remember to thank people for their time. I think people appreciate that." I pointed out that she also smiled in a genuine way, and she agreed: "Yes, I think I smile a lot."

It takes only one good interaction, one good conversation, to spark a connection with someone who can help you find a great job in the United States. You won't know when, where, or with whom these magical interactions will take place, so have as many conversations with as many people as possible. Take the initiative to create opportunities for yourself. Based on my experiences and observations, I don't believe international students are taking as much initiative as they should with reaching out to people.

Being too aggressive or too eager—borderline desperate—will not help, so ask for feedback from your mentors and your career advisor about how you come across. You don't want to seem nervous, rigid, or overly formal and shy. You want to come across as a socially savvy, polite, mature professional who is open and ready to make a difference in someone's business. That's what Americans are looking for. Follow the suggestions provided by Li Na. Her simple recipe for social savviness is a great starting point. Remember what she said:

"I just try to be myself. I try to be polite and sincere, and I try to remember to thank people for their time. I think people appreciate that."

And remember to smile. ☺

9

DEVELOP GREAT COMMUNICATION SKILLS WHEN YOUR ENGLISH IS JUST OK

Whoever is the best communicator gets the job! That's how it often seems to work in the United States. Strong communication is an essential skill to develop if you're trying to get a job in the United States. Can you clearly communicate your ideas to others? Are you able to influence your team members? Are you a good listener? When you speak, do others pay attention to you and feel connected to you? These are just some of the few questions you will need to find answers for as an international job seeker.

I have been asked many times: does securing a good job in the U.S. come down to "sounding good" when speaking? It does seem that way sometimes.

Good Communication = Competence

"People sometimes treat me like I don't know anything because I don't speak perfect English, but I'm a Ph.D. student who has published extensively in my field," an international student from Peru once told me.

This seems to be the world we live in when living in the United States: you'll likely need strong English skills to get noticed and receive credit for your achievements and talents. Speaking well translates to brain power. Strong communicators sometimes get hired into jobs they aren't fully qualified for, often beating other applicants with stronger work credentials but weaker communication skills. By speaking with the right speed, volume, and assertiveness, many candidates impress hiring managers by coming across as more competent than they actually are. If you are a strong communicator you have an advantage when job searching in the U.S. There's no question about that.

U.S. recruiters and hiring managers will expect nothing less than evidence that you can function in the United States with ease. At a minimum, they have to be able to understand you without trying too hard. Having an accent is totally okay—don't worry about that—but if people often have a tough time understanding you, that's going to be a problem, and you may be eliminated from the interview process. It's safe to describe most U.S. hiring managers as impatient. If you often need to have instructions or questions repeated to you because your English-language comprehension skills are not sufficiently strong, you will need to address this gap or you may not get hired.

Stories from the Office

While working as an MBA Career Coach for international students at the University of Maryland, when my office door was open, I often could not help overhearing what recruiters and hiring managers were saying about the students they interviewed. This was one of my favorite parts of my job: hearing firsthand, *in a completely spontaneous way*, what recruiters are saying about international students. On several occasions, I've heard, "This student is great, and I wish I could hire him, but his language skills aren't adequate. I couldn't really understand him with ease. We have to pass."

Language learning is like physical activity: it should be a lifelong commitment. You may think that being accepted into a U.S. university means your English is pretty good. But a TOEFL score of 100 or so doesn't necessarily mean you've mastered the level of language fluency that American managers are looking for. Your English skills will get better during your studies. As time goes on, you may even raise your hand from time to time to answer a question from one of your professors. That's all great news—except that you may not be improving fast enough. In the eyes of a recruiter, you may still not ready to work with Americans with ease and create strong relationships with them. Don't get a false sense of security regarding your language abilities. I've seen it happen too many times. You may think you've improved, and you probably have—but recruiters may be looking for more.

Get Help Now

Ask your career advisor the following questions:

- How do you feel about my language skills?

- Can I successfully interview for the types of jobs I'm interested in?

- Do you sometimes have a hard time understanding me?

- Should I focus on improving my language skills?

Ask for direct feedback. If you don't, you may spend your entire stay in the United States wondering why your job-search efforts were unsuccessful. Language could have been the reason, but nobody told you that was the case. Americans are direct communicators. They appreciate when you ask direct questions as well. Your English is probably better than you think. This is important to keep in mind as well since many international students are too tough on themselves. Know where you stand.

Can international students be great communicators even when, for many, English is their second language and communication is a highly cultural phenomenon? The answer is, yes, they can!

The most important soft skill for international students relates to the ability to communicate effectively, and this notion is different from speaking perfect English. I have seen many international students with average language skills secure great jobs in the United States. What was their secret, you may ask? They were open, not self-conscious about how they sounded, and they naturally invited others to want to interact with them.

Leveraging Your Language Limits

I once worked with a student from China named Zhang Wei who came to our university as an MBA with one of the best profiles in his incoming class: he had about seven years of credible work experience, including in-demand technical skills. Zhang Wei looked very strong on paper. Technology-consulting recruiters immediately gravitated toward him, and he secured interviews with big-name firms like Deloitte.

During one of his many interviews, a recruiter asked Zhang Wei what he thought his main barrier was going to be if hired. Zhang Wei immediately responded: language. The recruiter was probably already concerned that Zhang Wei might not have the needed level of language fluency necessary for the role he was seeking, and Zhang Wei simply confirmed her suspicion. In this particular case, Zhang Wei did not move forward in the interview cycle.

About a week after this interview, Zhang Wei scheduled an appointment to tell me how his interview went. He told me his remark about how language would be his main barrier if hired. While I appreciated his honesty and the recruiter surely did as well, I suggested that perhaps he'd missed an opportunity to turn what the recruiter already perceived as a weakness into a work-in-progress strength. He did not immediately understand what I was proposing. I asked for his thoughts on this alternate response:

> *I have greatly improved my English-language skills since I arrived in the United States, but I know there is much more work I need to do. I come from a country with a completely different alphabet, which is character-based. My English skills are getting better every day, and I can work with my American colleagues without much problem. But again, I know I must continue to improve.*

Zhang Wei said, "I love this! It's so true. You understand me. I can work well with others. Sometimes it's hard for me to say exactly what I want to say, but I can communicate."

I was happy to hear that Zhang Wei liked what I had proposed, but I was most happy that he firmly believed he could function and work in the United States despite the occasional language barriers we all knew he had.

My proposed statement reveals confidence and progress in an area that was challenging for Zhang Wei. Emphasizing progress would have helped Zhang Wei build his brand as a confident job applicant who is self-aware and has made an effort to improve. Zhang Wei missed an opportunity to turn what may have seemed like a liability into a positive character trait.

Smart job seekers always play to their strengths and turn a potential liability into a "good story" that can get them hired. Nobody is a perfect package. Remember that. If your language skills are not as great as you would like them to be, think of ways to position this aspect of your profile correctly.

Strategies to Implement

Remain open, friendly, and unselfconscious about your language skills so others will want to engage with you. That's key. Here are a few additional tips that are not hard to implement:

- Don't be so soft spoken that others have a tough time hearing you.

- Instead, speak loudly enough for others to hear you. This is often more important than worrying about speaking perfect English.

- Forget the pressure to be eloquent. Remember that you have a lot to say and contribute.

- Focus on the quality of your ideas and not so much on how you sound. Offer input often.

To improve your English language communication skills, do the following:

Hire a Tutor

I recently met an MS student from China who spoke good, clear, and natural English. I asked her, "What's your secret?" She said, "It all depends on how hard you want to push yourself." Pushing yourself is great, but do so with the help of a professional language tutor. The investment in language tutoring is well worth it if you're serious about getting a job in the United States, especially if you come from a non-English-speaking country and have had limited opportunities to practice your English. Group classes are not nearly as effective. One-on-one tutoring is best!

You might have wonderful pronunciation, but if you speak in a robotic monotone, your interactions with recruiters and hiring managers won't seem natural. Addressing potential challenges you may have, such as intonation and rhythm, is important, and a qualified tutor knows how to address these potential deficiencies.

Hire a language tutor before classes start. Once classes begin, you'll likely feel very overwhelmed—and there goes your best window of opportunity to hire a tutor. Walk over to your university's language or English for Speakers of Other Languages (ESOL) department and get information about hiring a qualified tutor. Ideally, hire a language tutor who has had experience working with students from your own country or region, as this individual will already be familiar with the specific types of language difficulties people from your country generally have.

Watch CNN, read the *Wall Street Journal*, or watch *Friends* to learn about language, culture, and humor. That's always helpful as well.

Find a Language Buddy

A language buddy is not a substitute for a professional tutor, but if you can find someone who is willing to meet you for coffee or lunch once a week or so to help you practice your English, that's great. Perhaps an American classmate who was once an international student will meet you at a Starbucks for some informal English conversation once a week. Don't worry about bothering people. Whoever ends up helping you will feel good about the opportunity to assist you, and they'll improve their own communication skills. It's a two-way process: you'll become confident by asking questions, and others will learn from you and become more in tune with how they communicate. Take the initiative, even if you feel a bit nervous. Practice with your advisor if needed.

Your language buddy may become your cultural mentor and help you adjust to life in the United States. It's nice to be able to ask questions about aspects of American life that you may feel unsure about; this will shorten your learning curve. In return, your cultural mentors gain a higher level of understanding of their own culture and yours. If you rely primarily on observation to figure out what's appropriate and what's not, you'll take too long to learn, and you may draw the wrong conclusions. Find someone in your class who seems friendly and say the following:

Hi. My name is Yang, and I'm from China. Do you mind if I sometimes ask you some questions about aspects of life in America that I'm not sure I completely understand?

Most people won't mind answering a few questions if you approach them correctly. Keep the request light and informal. It's about having fun and learning along the way.

Some international students have found "speaking clubs" helpful. Consider joining one if you have advanced English language skills. Toastmasters clubs seem very popular on U.S. college campuses. Do some research to see if your school has a chapter.

Don't Press "Send" Too Quickly

When it comes to written communication, I've seen emails and cover letters from international students addressed to recruiters and employers that are filled with grammar and spelling mistakes and whose tone is wrong. Though the most important thing is to improve your verbal communication skills, sharpen your written skills if you can as well. Consult with your school's writing studio and English-language center. Ask a friend to proofread critical written materials like resumes, emails, and cover letters if you are in the middle of the recruiting process.

Throw Yourself into Campus Life

You came to the United States to challenge yourself, right? If you're from Taiwan, why join the Asian student association when you can join the European or Latin American student association instead? You already know about life in your home country and region. Immerse yourself in something unfamiliar and create a college experience that will be memorable, will challenge you, and will help you be a more confident job seeker. Do something different.

No Roommate from Your Country

If you end up rooming with someone from your country, your ability to improve your language skills and become familiar with U.S. life will decrease. Many globally minded American students have told me that they would find it "soooo cool" to share an apartment or house with an international student.

Be brave! Ask your university to help you. Email the language department for suggestions on how to find an American roommate with an interest in the country you're from. A smart American student majoring in Japanese might love to have a roommate from Japan. If you haven't yet started classes, the admissions department might be able to assist as well.

Sign Up for a Fun Class with Americans Only

What do you like to do for fun? Are you ready to explore a new hobby? Take a dance class, a photography class, or any type of class that interests you that international students normally don't take. Interact with others who share your interests so you can learn from one another in a fun, relaxed way. You'll see how you'll suddenly start teaching others about something you know about and love. You're likely to make new friends and greatly improve your English in a spontaneous, natural way.

I grew up fishing and decided to take a fly-fishing class my first year in college in the United States. I was the only international student in it, and I was surrounded by American students who, like myself, liked to fish. I made new friends, greatly improved my language skills, and was introduced to some beautiful trout streams in Oregon by students who were happy to drive me around because I didn't have a car and didn't know where to go.

Volunteer at a Church, School, or Nursing Home

Help people. A couple of hours a week are all you need. Volunteering gives you a chance to experience America in a completely different way and improve your English at the same time. It can lead to great networking as well, of course, and you won't even know you're doing it. U.S.-based volunteer experience may give you talking points for an interview that a recruiter may be able to relate to more than, say, the contributions you made to a project at the bank you worked for in India or China before you came to the United States.

Get Off Campus

Consumed by classes and the demands of getting a degree overseas, few international students experience life beyond their college campuses, and that's a shame. Don't just talk with professors, students, or university staff. Get a different perspective on life in America by interacting with people from various backgrounds, outside of your university. Yelp and Meetup have several interest groups ranging from camping to cooking to job hunting. Join one. Go with a friend one day. Once you get more comfortable, go alone and make some new friends. Always use good judgment but don't be afraid to get out there.

Learn How to Be Succinct

This is tough! When speaking a language other than your own, it is possible to feel a little lost and out of control. This lack of control usually translates into being wordy. You want just the opposite: you want to be succinct. Americans can be impatient. They like when you "cut to the chase." Americans usually don't like when people ramble. When explaining what you do or want to do professionally, *one sentence* is enough. Learn how to briefly tell people what you can do for them. I once worked with a student from India who came to see me right before an MBA career fair because he wanted to carefully choose the right *keywords* to use when speaking with recruiters. How smart of him. Essentially, he was working on his self-promotion sound bite. He came up with this statement:

> *I'm a gadget enthusiast who can turn technology into revenue streams for companies.*

Simplify so anyone you meet understands what you want to do, whether they work in your desired field or not. Don't waste words. Be crisp.

121

Because the question "What kind of work are you interested in?" will come up often, it pays off to think ahead.

Coming up with a powerful value proposition statement can be much harder than working on your resume. A resume gives you an entire page, and now you have to condense an entire page of work history into a *single simple sentence* that represents who you are and your potential value to employers. The right choice of words makes all the difference. It takes time and help to generate an effective statement, particularly if English is not your first language. Limit your statement to no more than 15 words. My statement is the following:

> *I help international students convert disadvantages into advantages that get them hired.*

If your statement is effective, others will respond, "Wow. That's interesting. Tell me more. How do you do that?"

What is *your* statement?

_____

_____

10

INTERVIEWING ON YOUR TERMS

"We live in an age of desperation. Never in living memory has the competition for job openings been more intense. Never have job interviews been tougher. This is the bitter fruit of the jobless recovery and the changing nature of work."

Excerpt from *Are You Smart Enough to Work at Google?* by
William Poundstone

Many dynamics arise during an interview that might be difficult for international students to manage. For instance, American employers will want you to speak confidently about yourself and your successes. If you don't, they may question how strong your communication skills are, your ability to influence others, your confidence, and even how competent you might be. "A little bit of bragging is sometimes okay," confirms an alumnus who provided interview tips to the students at our university. These are scary expectations for many international students who are not used to talking about themselves, let alone feeling comfortable promoting their qualifications to others. Self-promotion is uncommon and even rude in many cultures. Many international students come across as too humble and underwhelming when interviewing for U.S. positions.

So what do you do?

The United States is perhaps the most overtly self-promotional country in the world.

Overall, American professionals and college students are quite comfortable promoting themselves, especially in a business environment — as this behavior is actively encouraged as a sign of competence and self-confidence during interviews.

International students forget—perhaps because they aren't reminded enough—that although an interview is kind of a "test," it's also, and perhaps most importantly, a *conversation*. Take a minute to think about a couple of instances when you had a great conversation with someone. Did you have to pretend to be someone you were not?

Did you have to act in any kind of way that made you really uncomfortable? Probably not. You were yourself. And as a good listener you also remained focused on connecting with whomever you were speaking with. Consciously or unconsciously, whether an intentional effort was made or not, if both parties feel the conversation was great, it was because they were able to be who they are with each other, and the conversation naturally flowed. It found its rhythm. Neither party was really trying.

An interview may not be quite like a chat you have with a friend on a Friday evening at a bar, but there are many similarities. At the end of a great chat, or at the end of great interview, both parties need to feel that they just had a great conversation. Don't be naïve, though: when interviewing, as a candidate you must clearly understand what recruiters and hiring managers are looking for.

There are many interview formats, and each industry and job category may have its own specific interview dynamics you will need to learn about. Your career center will work with you to help you become comfortable answering different interview questions. You will likely learn about the STAR format: situation, task, action, result. When working with international students, I modify the STAR format slightly to include one additional element, emotion, to form the STARE format. Here is a brief explanation of the STARE format:

- Situation: What was the situation you faced?

- Task: What tasks were involved in that situation?

- Action: What actions did you take?

- Results: What were the results of those actions?

- **Emotion:** How did it feel for you to be involved in this situation?

The E portion of the STARE format does not need to come at the end of your story. It can be incorporated in each of the previous sections of your STAR answer.

Fang Wang's Story

For several months, I'd been working with Fang Wang, the student from China I introduced in the first paragraph of the book. Fang Wang was getting her MBA. After considering finance as a possible track, she discovered marketing analytics and decided to focus on that. One of the first things I noticed about Wang was how confident she felt ruling out possible career choices. "I took the time to understand what was available and moved a little slowly," she told me.

A strong student with great math skills, she knew what she was good at and what areas she did not excel in. Numbers were her thing. Talking with people and highlighting her strengths—not so much. She came to our university with one of the highest GMAT scores in her class (740), and she continued to excel academically during her studies.

With a clear sense of what she wanted to do professionally, she had to find the right roles to apply for and the right companies to network with. She left no stone unturned. While many of her MBA colleagues didn't bother attending our university-wide career fair because the event was mainly geared toward undergraduate students and few "MBA-grade jobs" had been advertised, Fang Wang thought it was worth her time to go so she could network with healthcare companies that might have interesting roles for her in the future. In the United States, we call Fang Wang a hustler.

Pleasant to talk to, quiet, and low-key, Fang Wang was fairly unknown among the other career coaches on my team. Her communication skills were pretty decent. When I first met with her, she was able to effortlessly articulate to me what she thought her main job-search challenges were: "I can't sell myself. I don't interview well. Maybe I won't get a job in the United States."

She scheduled a few additional appointments to try to improve her elevator pitch and her overall ability to sell herself during interviews. She was excited about an upcoming interview with a healthcare firm.

At first, I agreed that Fang Wang may come across as very underwhelming when interviewing. At times, she seemed completely unable to draw any attention to her skills. Her answers were short and generally not very impactful. It almost felt like she didn't want to be talking. Her responses to my mock interview questions completely lacked emotion; any good conversation—and any good interview—must have at least some emotion. I thought to myself, "You're right. You may not get a job in the

United States unless we can figure something out." In my mind I had labeled Fang Wang as someone who was not very expressive. It seemed to be the right conclusion.

What was keeping Fang Wang from interviewing with a little bit more confidence? Was it language? Was it culture? Was it her personality? Was it a combination of all of these factors? Her English was above average, so I ruled language out. Unable to find a satisfactory answer, I asked Wang herself what she thought could be the root cause of her interview challenges.

"It's really not my English, I don't think," she said. "Maybe it's because I have limited work experience compared to my classmates. I'm not sure." I wasn't sure, either. While I appreciated Wang's answer, her insights didn't help me too much. I tried to troubleshoot the situation but didn't get very far.

Preparing for the Interviews

I wanted to prepare Fang Wang the best I could for her interviews, including a final round of interviews for an exciting marketing analytics position with a local healthcare company that seemed perfect for her. During one of our mock interviews, I asked her, "What's so intriguing about marketing analytics? Why do you like this part of marketing so much?" She responded without hesitation, "The numbers just make sense in my head, and I like the challenge of looking at what's behind the numbers. Analytics isn't just math."

This was a very strong opening, the best I'd heard her deliver. I loved what she'd said, but it still wasn't the homerun I thought she needed. I wanted to better understand what Wang meant when she told me that the numbers "make sense in her head," so I asked her this question: "Do you have anything you can show me, perhaps an analysis you have done for one of your classes, that would help me understand the kind of work you like doing?"

"I can show you assignments I turned in for my forecasting class. I think the job I found requires similar skills," she said, and handed over the models. Wow! Fang Wang made data modeling look easy. Her algorithms and formulas seemed to have a 3D quality. They were beautifully simple, yet captured the complexity of the business scenarios she was asked to evaluate. As part of her homework, she'd been given disparate data sets to play with, and her job was to generate a forecasting model that predicted the future sales of a cereal positioned to compete against Kellogg's products. The first thing Wang showed me was how she combined the three different data sets into a single Excel file. Her work was so logical and "clean" it took me 15 seconds to understand what she had done. "How long did it take you to do this?" I asked her. "Two hours," she said. "I would have been up all night *trying* to merge the disparate files," I told her.

The best part of reviewing these assignments was seeing Fang Wang's spontaneity and pride when describing what she had produced. It was a breath of fresh air, an incredible performance precisely because Wang was not "on." I was engaged the entire time. Fang Wang was completely comfortable telling me what she'd done, why she'd made the decisions she'd made, and why she thought the correlations she'd found in the data set were not that surprising after all.

Reviewing Fang Wang's work helped me forget for a moment that I was there to coach her or "fix" her.

As I better understood the power of her skill set and the impact she could have as a worker, I remember thinking, "One lucky manager out there will hire Fang Wang, and he or she will be very happy."

Focus on What You Offer

In theory, a company will not offer you a great salary and hire you because you have great interviewing skills per se. Many applicants can smoothly respond to inquiries like "Walk me through your resume" or "Tell me about yourself." But when you peel the onion apart, so to speak, the middle is empty. A close inspection of their track record may reveal that they have not lived up to the flawless interview performance that got them hired. Their polished answers and charm captivated their interviewers, though, and they got on payroll, sometimes for the wrong reasons. This method of getting hired works for many people. Typically, it's not a strategy that has proven to be effective for many international students due to linguistic and cultural reasons, as well as a variety of other factors.

In theory, companies will hire you because you're a strong problem solver, someone who can add creativity to new product designs, someone who can fix a supply-chain issue to accelerate the delivery of products to market, someone who can conduct a strong financial analysis of a potential acquisition, or someone who can generate models to predict future product sales. Interviews will give you a chance to communicate your skills and experiences in a way that demonstrates their transferability to the job you're seeking. Find a comfortable way to do that. Your job isn't to interview well per se: it's to show those you're talking to that you can generate value for them. There may be a multitude of different ways for you to accomplish that, *on your terms*.

Interviewing Strategies

Before we continue to review Fang Wang's interview experience and preparation, take a look at some interview strategies that are of particular importance to international students:

- Take a moment to think about your responses before you speak. You may need a bit more time to process a question and gather your thoughts. It's okay to pause for two or three seconds before you answer. Just make sure that the length of the pause doesn't make the interviewer uncomfortable. Practice with your advisor. Buying yourself a few seconds before answering a question can be very helpful. It's also a sign that you think before you speak.

- Are you talking too fast? Probably. Practice speaking slowly. Some international students talk too fast, particularly in stressful situations like interviewing. Learn how to speak slowly—it's a sign of control, and it often helps people more easily understand you.

- Practice informality. International students tend to be too formal during interviews. Many international students are used to a more formal professional environment. Much of this formality is rooted in culture and/or linguistics—or, sometimes, nervousness. Remember to relax. Try to enjoy the moment and create an environment where your conversation can be relaxed and enjoyable.

- Again, it's a conversation. Remember that when interviewing. From a delivery standpoint, your words must flow like normal conversation. From a strategy standpoint, you must find a way to showcase your skills to employers in a manner that is natural to you.

- If you're confused by a question, it's okay to say, "Could you please clarify your question? I didn't quite understand what you said," and hope the interviewer will ask the question in a different way. Seeking clarification for language reasons is not ideal, since it could raise red flags about your language ability, but it's much better than providing an answer that doesn't match the question. Ask for clarification more than once or twice, however, and you may be out of the contest.

- If you struggle with specific English words or sounds—as I do—avoid using them during an interview. Occasionally a word pops into my brain that my mouth and tongue are not ready to say correctly. What do I do? I discard it and look for a synonym. Choose words you can say with confidence. Your English tutor will help you recognize specific English sounds that trip you up. For example, the word "specificity" is difficult for me to pronounce correctly, but I can say "precision" with no problem. If you mispronounce a word, just move on. It will happen. It's really not a big deal. You can even laugh at yourself. Remember that self-confidence is critical.

- You will receive specific questions about your skills and competency. Answer questions in a direct way. As we discussed earlier, remember how Americans are most comfortable communicating. Don't leave the interviewer guessing what you're good at. Demonstrate self-awareness and self-confidence. You can soften what you're saying with phrases like "I *believe* I am good at..." or "I *feel* I excel in ..." An appropriate statement might be:

  I feel I am quite strong with JavaScript. Programming comes easily to me. My peers tell me I am fast, and for the most part my code is bug-free. I'd be happy to show you some samples of my work.

- When given the opportunity to ask questions, consider a few categories that are of particular interest for international students. Innovation is an elusive idea but one that international students can positively impact because of their unique background. Another interesting area to mine for thoughtful questions is growth. These days, growth is often tied to international investments and sometimes acquisitions, which are areas in which the background of international students can shine. You should be able to speak intelligently about these topics.

- Formulate a strategy. Choose ahead of time two or three key messages you want to convey to the interviewer. At a minimum, you know that you will have to show the connections between what you have done previously and the role you want, show evidence that you can successfully perform the duties of the role you are applying for, and show that you fit.

- Partner with your career coach to generate interview strategies that account for variables like your command of English, your understanding of U.S. culture, the role you're interviewing for, and what you'll be graded on when interviewing.

A Career Advisor's Help

Back to Fang Wang's interview preparation. Instead of spending time and effort helping Wang become a stronger interviewer, I took a different approach to help her generate better results. Fang Wang lacked the communication assertiveness that U.S. recruiters like to see, particularly in MBA hires—or so I thought. My concerns were valid: she was targeting roles that required extensive cross-functional work. She would be explaining abstract concepts to people all the time. She needed to project confidence in her ideas. I was afraid that great data modeling skills were not going to be enough.

Judged by U.S. standards, Fang Wang was not even an average interviewer. After a few meetings I was under no illusion that she should prepare for her interviews the conventional way. Nevertheless, I wasn't sure what strategies she should utilize. I did know that many international students are quite uncomfortable with "American-style" self-promotion; many feel that unless they sell themselves correctly during interviews, they won't get hired. Self-promotion is often misunderstood by international students, who link it to being aggressive and showing value at all times. Many cringe at the phrase "elevator pitch" and internalize the thought that unless they do a good job "selling themselves" during interviews, they won't get hired.

I decided that my job was to help Fang Wang determine how she could best convey her skills and value in a way that respected her background and limitations. I had labeled Wang as inexpressive. What a mistake! Expressing herself in cognitive ways—typical for many international students—was how Wang had been wired to function. By luck, she and I figured out how she needed to prepare—or not prepare—for her upcoming interview.

Changing the Nature of "Self-Promotion"

Fang Wang and I discussed the possibility of walking her interviewer through the homework samples she had reviewed with me. Meticulous and bright, she had great pride in the models she'd produced for one of her classes, and those served as good evidence of her professional capabilities as they related to the job she was applying for.

"But how's the interviewer going to know I even worked on those assignments?" she asked me.

"He won't," I said. "But there might be moments during the interview where you can say, 'May I share with you some modeling work I've done for one of my classes that I feel is relevant for the role we're discussing?'"

She was clearly not sold. Wang told me she didn't know that volunteering to share samples of her work was an available option. She was skeptical. We role-played different ways to handle the situation, and while she was not immediately excited about my suggestion, she slowly warmed up to the idea. Eventually, on her own, she came to view the interview process as an opportunity to let the interviewer get a glimpse of the type of work she could produce if hired. The quality of her work was clear. When Wang shifted her focus to explaining something tangible that she had produced, she shone without trying. She communicated.

To ease her anxiety, I explained that some interviews are highly structured; the interviewer(s) will lead the way and, in theory, will ask all candidates the same questions so they can be compared with one another. I told her that it was very possible that her interviewer would say Wang didn't need to share any samples of her work, and that she shouldn't feel awkward if that happened. Finally, I advised Wang to read the interview situation and then decide if it was appropriate to offer samples of her work. She was on board with this vision. We decided that toward the end of her interview, when recruiters usually give interviewees a chance to ask questions, she could offer to share samples of her work.

I prayed that she would be given a chance to review her forecasting models. I thought that would tilt the balance in her favor. If the interviewer did not provide her with this opportunity, we decided we'd include her homework assignments as part of her thank-you note after the interview. The message would look something like this:

Dear Mr. John Smith:

I enjoyed the conversation we had today and feel the role we discussed fits me well. Attached to this email you will find some modeling work I completed for one of my classes. I thought I would share these files with you as samples of the kind of work I might be able to produce for your firm. I would be delighted to review the attached with you.

Sincerely,

Fang Wang

I couldn't wait to hear how Fang Wang's interview went. When I saw her the next day, I asked if she'd had the chance to review her models with her interviewer. "I did, and it went well. It didn't feel like I was selling. I was just explaining," she said.

Wang's written offer came a couple of days later. She got her dream job at a high-growth, mid-size technology healthcare company, in her field of interest, doing work that fully leveraged her background. Wang was on her way to becoming an H-1B worker.

Success!

An introvert who could not sell herself, Fang Wang slowly learned that like everyone else in the world, she had strengths and weaknesses. Even after two years of graduate school, many international students still lack U.S. levels of communication assertiveness and self-confidence that they believe are needed to conduct great interviews. Fang Wang may never become a great interviewee by U.S. standards, but that won't stop her from succeeding and securing quality jobs if she finds creative ways to showcase her capabilities to her future employer.

Her initial mindset is typical of the many international students I have tried to help over the years: pressured to prepare for interviews the traditional way, and convinced they need to get better at selling themselves, international students end up executing interview strategies that were never designed to accommodate them. The result? They come across as rigid, robotic, and stiff—adjectives I have often heard U.S. recruiters use to describe international students. In the meantime, American recruiters are looking for candidates who can intelligently and comfortably talk about their lives and professional experiences, and how these relate to the role they're interested in.

If you interview well, that's great. If you're an average interviewee who wants to work hard to improve your interviewing skills, go for it. Sharing samples of your work won't always save you. Other times you may need more than that. If, like Wang, you interview below U.S. standards, sometimes shifting your focus from improving according to interview frameworks that don't suit you to generating new interview strategies that *do* suit you and that you can execute with confidence is the smart route to take.

Don't ever let employers underestimate the intellectual and strategic resource—the raw intelligence—that you as an international worker can bring to their firms.

11

THE GREATEST GIFT OF ALL: BECOMING BICULTURAL

For many international students, learning to effortlessly speak the language of their host country is one of the main perks of studying abroad. But if you bought this book, you expect much more for yourself: you are a career-driven individual who wants a great job in the United States after graduation. Perhaps the biggest benefit of studying and living overseas, one that is not immediately recognized by international students, is the amazing chance to become bicultural or sometimes multicultural, a trait that can not only help you get a great job but ultimately make you incredibly successful.

Being bilingual does not mean being bicultural: these are very different things. Bicultural citizens have the ability to see what's happening around them through the lenses of their own culture, the country they grew up in, and their new host country. What could be more interesting and powerful? Becoming bicultural should be one of the main goals for international students. Those who immerse themselves in their new community will start a journey that will transform them forever and create amazing career-growth opportunities along the way.

Like learning a new language, becoming bicultural is not quick or easy, but it can be fun—and it will permanently change you.

The Perks

The perks of being bicultural are many:

- Life is a lot more interesting and fun when you have the ability to interpret it in different ways.

- Being bicultural will give you an edge in the job-search process throughout your career.

- Being bicultural will create amazing networking opportunities for you, both personal and professional. It's cool to be international.

- As for personal growth, being bicultural will force you to be introspective and learn a great deal about yourself, the world, and business.

We need more bicultural individuals in the world because they are capable of evaluating problems, opportunities, and conflicts with different perspectives. Too many individuals are set in their own ways because they don't know anything different. They have experienced only one reality. As an international student, you probably speak other languages and have traveled. You have considerable empathy for people with different views. International students have been exposed to so much more, and they can be very valuable to U.S. employers.

The question, of course, is whether employers care if you're bicultural. And if they don't, how can you still leverage your bicultural background during your job search? Unfortunately, recruiters and hiring managers may not immediately appreciate or understand how powerful it can be to have a bicultural worker on their team. They may never have spent a meaningful amount of time outside the United States themselves, so they may not be able to see the unique benefits that someone with global fluency could bring to their firm.

The Research

The topic of biculturalism has been of interest to academics. Research shows that bicultural employees are characterized by greater creativity and professional success, and that the major breakthroughs in history have come from those who challenged conventional thinking. You have to feel confident positioning yourself as a different kind of hire, because that's who you are. There are some interesting studies that highlight just how special bicultural individuals can be.

Biculturals Are Creative

In one particular study[1], MBA students at a large business school in Europe who had lived abroad for an average of four years were given a creative-uses task. They were shown a picture of a brick and had two minutes to write down as many creative uses of it as they could think of. When three components of creativity were examined, the biculturals exhibited more fluency (they generated more ideas), more flexibility (they generated a greater number of ideas), and more novelty (they were more creative in their suggestions).

As an international student, you're capable of looking at a brick and imagining various uses for it. You're capable of a kind of creativity that others may not have. Employers are looking for individuals who can think outside the box, and if you can show your interviewers how your fresh ideas can help them grow their business, you'll get noticed.

"Creativity is every company's first driver," claims Nolan Bushnell, founder of Atari and Chuck E. Cheese's, in his book, *Finding the Next*

---

[1] The results of the tests administered to bilingual participants highlighted in this chapter are fully explained in a paper called "Getting the Most Out of Living Abroad: Biculturalism and Integrative Complexity as Key Drivers of Creative and Professional Success" (Tadmor, Galinsky, & Maddux, 2012). The authors performed three different studies and compared the test results of participants who are and are not bicultural.

Steve Jobs. Whether you're manufacturing iPhones, designing the next hot mobile app, or designing a new building to add to the existing skyline of a city, it's imperative that you exercise a high level of creativity. You have to blow open your business model—if you don't, someone else will. The only way to stay ahead is to anticipate and entertain new concepts, products, and ideas. Your challenge, no matter what industry or job you're targeting, is to show that you do think differently, and that your fresh ideas mean value for the firms you want to join. Create situations where others can learn from your unique insights.

For businesses to grow, they need to adapt and learn how to do things differently. Innovation is often required but hard to find. A different perspective is often needed no matter what kind of work or industry you want to join.

Everyone is looking for fresh thinking. Every company, no matter how large or small, should be trying to hire the next Steve Jobs. Everyone is looking more or less for the same traits in the business world: technical depth; ability to make sense of disparate data sets; creative problem solving; and, of course, the communication skills needed to run with ideas, engage others, and bring visions to reality. International students often have many of the characteristics that employers have a hard time finding in candidates who have not been exposed to life outside their own country.

Exercise your uniqueness, intelligence, and fresh thinking and watch hiring managers fall in love with you because you're nothing like the seven candidates they interviewed before you.

Biculturals Bring Innovation

In the second study, the researchers examined how biculturalism affects real-world innovations in a group of MBA students at a U.S. business school. Again, the participants had lived abroad and came from different countries. The study examined how many new businesses the participants had started, how many novel products or services they had invented, and how many breakthrough process innovations they had created. Guess what the results were? Biculturals once again did better than the other participants.

None of these findings surprise me. I see the creativity of the international students I work with every day, and I often recommend that they utilize a statement like this when speaking with U.S. recruiters and hiring managers:

> *As a bicultural individual, I have the ability to analyze problems and issues from a different perspective. I think I can bring a level of creative thinking into your company that could open new doors to help your organization grow. Let me give you a specific example ...*

Be bold. Be specific. Get noticed. Get hired.

Biculturals Are Successful

Finally, in the third study, the researchers asked whether being bicultural leads to professional success (as measured by the rate of managerial advancement), and to an increase in managerial reputation (as judged by peers). This time, the participants were Israeli professionals in the United States who had worked on the West Coast, primarily in Silicon Valley, for slightly more than eight years on average. The researchers found that biculturals achieved higher promotion rates and had more positive reputations than those who were not bicultural.

The authors of the study further concluded that biculturals have the "capacity and willingness to acknowledge the legitimacy of competing perspectives on the same issue." If you are already in the United States as an international student, when sitting in class listening to your professors, you may have already noticed that you are able to intuitively combine multiple perspectives when analyzing a situation. Your bicultural brain is working in different ways, which you may not even realize. Pay attention to what's happening. Often you can repurpose old ideas and concepts, combine them with some other ideas, and create something new.

Bicultural Job Hunters

By now you should realize that you have unique cultural advantages that can be true differentiators in your job search. The fact that you were born and raised outside of the United States can be an advantage. Some of these advantages cannot be easily duplicated by your competition. Being international—and, ideally, bicultural—is itself a huge advantage, but you may need strong marketing skills and tight storytelling skills to get recruiters to recognize and appreciate your unique talents and perspectives. That's why the recommendation and frameworks presented on Chapter 6, "Sharing Your Story," are so important.

International students' work ethic, intelligence, and thoughtfulness are admirable characteristics, but they're only the tip of the iceberg. They are only the most obvious aspects of the profile of an international individual sought after by U.S. firms.

Who, in theory, are the best problem solvers? People who can look at issues through multiple perspectives and at times help companies avoid costly mistakes. Consider the following example.

My country, Brazil, now attracts the attention of the world's biggest brands. Nike, for example, wanted a strong showing in Brazil during and after the 2014 World Cup. They hired Mandalah consultant Lourenço Bustani, who warned Nike about what Brazilians feared the most: being abandoned after the World Cup and the Olympics. Together with Nike, Bustani co-created a vision for the brand that went beyond making a few bucks from the World Cup and focused on understanding sport as a perennial catalyst for integration between a city's residents. Bustani could do this because he knows the dynamics of the Brazilian market so deeply; and, since he was educated in the United States, he also knows how American companies tend to think about branding and the mistakes they're likely to make when venturing into unfamiliar territories.

Bustani was able to help *redefine* Nike's branding approach effectively because he's multi-cultural. He has a foot in both worlds—the United States and his home country, Brazil—which allows him to offer insights and suggestions that others cannot. Like Bustani, if you can bridge two cultures, no matter what field or type of work you're interested in, and you can help organizations adapt and win in the marketplace by proposing business tactics that take into account hidden market complexities that only someone with your international background is able to see, you win. Often it takes a multi-cultural individual—like an international student —to generate this kind of unique insight.

Successful marketers have a global perspective and know how to manage product launches and gain market share in emerging world regions. Who is best equipped for these types of jobs? You are. International students are.

I asked Lourenço, who receives resumes from graduates from top U.S universities interested in working at Mandalah, to share some advice with international students who are thinking about jobs and careers. This is what he had to say:

"My advice is to focus more on your vitae and less on your curriculum, or at least to find a better balance between the two. The challenges businesses are facing today have less to do with the kinds of skill sets and technical competencies you learn in the classroom and more to do with how you see and interact with the world around you. Get out of your comfort zone and travel, pick up a new language, absorb a new culture and dive into a different tradition. After all, you are a product of the people and the places that live within you. The more ample your repertoire, the more apt you will be to serve those around you, creatively and courageously."

Differentiate Yourself

When you apply for quality jobs where you will be facing intense competition, embrace your multi-cultural identity and describe what is unique about you in specific ways. Those who are fortunate enough to experience more than one culture may develop cognitive abilities that others don't have. Don't be afraid to differentiate. Don't go down the standard route. Lourenço didn't and that is one of the reasons he got noticed. You are capable of much more. Beyond the obvious qualities and traits you can offer to employers, such as global mobility, language skills, knowledge of your home region, and deep technical or quantitative expertise, as a multicultural worker showcase unique and interesting insights about whatever field you're interested in. This powerful combination of abilities and traits can make U.S. employers salivate over you.

International students have a unique opportunity to fuse the unique competencies and strengths they acquired at home with the knowledge and awareness they've absorbed while working and studying overseas. That's not always easy to do, though. When we study and work overseas, it's easy to only apply concepts that our host country considers "acceptable." As an international student, it's tempting to start repeating the knowledge contained in your American textbooks. If you do that too much, you'll start sounding like everybody else, because education forces people to think in ways that society has dictated. Don't let your newly acquired U.S. knowledge blind you. Combine it with knowledge and experiences you brought with you from your home country and the general awareness you have about the world. With a foot in two different worlds, you can generate insights and recommendations that others cannot. It's not just about an infusion of new ideas. Sometimes it's about a different way of linking concepts that may already exist.

Professionals with know-how and insights about emerging markets are more needed than ever. The development of a stronger middle class in several countries has required U.S firms to structure themselves differently. For instance, when large Western companies rushed to enter emerging markets 20 years ago, they tended to gear their products to small segments of buyers, many of whom were used to traveling to the United States and sometimes lived an American lifestyle at home; people who could have been approached by using conventional Western marketing tactics. The opportunities are much greater now, but so are the challenges. It's not easy to develop an unbiased understanding of the purchasing behavior, unique characteristics, and needs of new consumers in developing countries. It's tough to pick up on critical nuances by reading a couple of books. Globally minded individuals who are able to get into the psyche of a growing middle class of consumers will be needed to crack the code in a variety of different industries and functions.

Getting Smart By Hanging Out With International Students

It seems that American students who spend time with international students pick up new tricks along the way. David Jamieson-Drake and Jiali Luo, who are directors of research at Duke University, interviewed American alumni from three separate graduating classes who considered themselves highly interactive with international students. They discovered that American students challenged their own belief systems when they had spent a considerable amount of time with international students. In addition, they had acquired a number of practical skills and qualities, including better computer capability, ability to learn new languages, and ability to acquire new skills independently.

It seems that the same type of knowledge transfer could continue to take place at the enterprise level as well, once international students join the U.S. workforce.

Benefits for Organizations

There are tangible benefits for organizations who hire those who are culturally different. New models of everything are needed, no matter what industry or functional area you're trying to break into. In plain English: innovation is required, and fresh and insightful thinking gets you noticed. Workers who are able to harvest the best of both worlds—their old world at home, and their new world in the United States—in creative and sustained ways, while fighting the natural tendency to fit in and conform, are workers that smart companies will want to hire. Smart companies will appreciate their differences and encourage them to exercise their unique out-of-the-box thinking while remaining true to who they are. As an international student looking for a job, you are uniquely positioned to create unbeatable combinations and delivering a differentiated message to U.S. recruiters and hiring managers.

Multicultural citizens get better job opportunities and a cognitive boost that allows them to be creative problem solvers and interesting individuals, *both* of which are traits highly valued by U.S hiring managers. As an international job seeker looking for a great professional opportunity in the U.S. the secret is to capitalize on these characteristics by providing tangible evidence of how your superior brain power translates into value for the firms you are targeting.

12

THE BIG, BAD VISA CHAPTER

Information in this chapter should not be considered legal advice, and international students are cautioned to consult legal counsel to discuss the most current immigration law issues that could impact their careers in the U.S.

Here it is, the subject international students lose sleep over, visas. Such a little word, such big worries. From the time you decide to study abroad, you'll be dealing with visa matters—some easy, some challenging, some you have no control over, and all important to your future in the United States. At the time this book went to press, there were 85,000 H-1B visas available. Each chapter in this book is meant to help you get closer to securing an H-1B visa for yourself.

In order to address visa questions, career centers across the country often bring immigration attorneys to campus to present up-to-date information on visa matters to international students. These sessions tend to be well attended and often receive very positive reviews from students. I've attended several of these workshops over the years, and I can clearly see how engaged international students are in the subject. There's usually no laughter in the room. The tone is usually very serious. Some students take notes nonstop. The expressions on their faces say it all: this content is critical. I need to learn and know this stuff in order to find a job.

The Myth of Required Expertise

While researching articles and publications geared toward helping international students find employment in the United States, I came across one that encouraged students to become *experts* on their visa situation. The premise behind the recommendation is that it will help international students be more confident when applying for jobs.

If this is true, then the anxiety international students feel over knowing everything they can about visas makes sense. I've had students book appointments with me because they felt they needed to be experts on the topic of work visas, particularly the H-1B. An international student from China once told me he felt that he was at a *disadvantage* compared to other international students looking for a job because he didn't know as much about the H-1B visa process as his peers did. I reassured him that he needed to know the basics of the H-1B visa process, such as quota release and basic eligibility rules, but he did *not* need to be an expert. He remained unconvinced and said, "I think it's best I learn as much as I can."

The notion that international students must educate prospective employers on visa matters in order to secure a job in the United States is usually what drives this kind of anxiety. Many international students believe that those who are skilled at educating employers about visa rules have a better chance of getting hired than those who aren't.

Take It from a Career Coach

This is what I have learned over the years:

- I have yet to meet one international student who went home after graduation who felt that he or she didn't get a job in the United States because of a lack of knowledge about the H-1B visa.

- No recruiter who's hired an international student has ever told me that the student's ability to speak and answer questions about the visa-sponsorship process gave him or her an edge over other candidates.

- Similarly, I've never met a single recruiter who told me that the reason an international student wasn't chosen for a position was because the candidate didn't seem to know enough about the visa process, or couldn't answer a question about the H-1B visa that came up during an interview.

In this chapter, what I propose is that we keep the quest for visa knowledge *in perspective*.

Remember this: most companies will check with an immigration attorney if they're serious about hiring you. An experienced attorney will correctly file your application. Don't feel you need to be an expert on visas—there are experts out there already, eager to help, and how to engage them to assist you with visa matters during your job search is what I will teach you in this chapter.

You need to know enough about the H-1B sponsorship process to make those you're talking to comfortable with the possibility of hiring you. But you need to become an expert on your value proposition and how to communicate that to an employer. That's what you need to focus on. This needs to be your main priority. Never lose sight of that. When people like you and understand your value, a visa won't be a big deal anymore.

Believing that knowledge about visas and U.S. immigration will make you a more competitive job seeker creates a dangerously false sense of security for international students. Many fall victim to this anxiety and fail to apply maximum energy and focus on developing other critical job-search skills, such as networking and interviewing. The amount of focus placed on visa matters can sometimes be highly disproportionate to what the topic deserves. Some employers routinely sponsor international candidates; others never do; and some fall somewhere in the middle. You need to understand your audience. Never forget the foundation of a successful job search: demonstrating the impact of your skills and passions to prospective employers. That's what gets you hired.

I'm not suggesting that you ignore visas entirely. That's not the message. Depending on the situation, you may indeed need to know the basics of the visa process so at times you can address employers' concerns about sponsorship. The important thing is how you have these conversations, and this is what we'll focus on.

H-1B Visa Basics

Although the H-1B visa isn't the only work visa, it's the most common work visa for international students, so it's what we'll focus on here. The quota for H-1B visas allows for 65,000 approvals for anyone with a bachelor's degree or higher from anywhere in the world, and 20,000 approvals for foreign nationals holding a U.S. advanced degree (master's degree or higher). Assuming you meet the eligibility requirements, H-1B visas are for *anyone*, not just for computer science or engineering majors. You could major in journalism, biology, or literature and secure an H-1B visa.

If you are determined to stay in the United States after graduation, your odds of securing an H-1B are greater if you have a U.S. master's degree. The 20,000 visas allocated to those who have a U.S. master's degree or higher (no undergraduates allowed) are worth gold. The probability of your employer being able to secure an H-1B visa for you as a master's student is unknown, because the government does not disclose how many of the H-1B filings were for undergraduate students and how many were for master's students. But the odds are in your and your employer's favor. Based on the laws of probability and data from recent years, you will probably secure an H-1B visa if you have a master's degree or higher from a U.S school.

Increasing Your Odds with the Visa Lottery

Regarding increasing your odds with the visa lottery, the best situation for international students is securing a job before the filing deadline while you're still in school. Let's say you get hired by company X in March during your senior year, or your last year of graduate school. Company X has the opportunity to file for your H-1B April 1, while you're still in school. If you get your H-1B, that's great. If you don't get it, no need to get too worried, because you can start your job using OPT and reapply for your H-1B the following year. *This is a great situation to be in.* In this scenario, assuming you don't get your H-1B the first time you apply for it, you'll have a chance to participate in the lottery the following year, therefore increasing your odds.

Good (Excellent) H-1B News for International Students

Good news—about the H-1B visa? Really? It may seem that filing for an H-1B visa is a distant, unlikely dream. You may find yourself with this thought first and foremost in your mind:

> *I've heard that employers need to prove that no U.S. worker was available to apply for a job before hiring an international student and providing the student with an H–1B. Is this true?*

This is not true. Are you jumping up and down right now? You should be. Employers don't need to prove to anyone that they couldn't find a U.S. citizen who was willing and/or qualified to accept the job you're being offered. In fact, an employer doesn't even need to interview any U.S. citizens before making you an offer. This is true for any field of work. This often-unknown fact opens the door for further conversations with just about any employer.

The Root of the Confusion

The confusion around whether employers need to "justify" your employment usually comes from existing regulations associated with the green-card process (permanent residency), where such requirements do exist. When talking to U.S. recruiters or hiring managers, if you sense they think that they need to justify to the U.S. government that no U.S. citizen was able to take the H-1B job they want to offer you, be sure to clarify for them that they do not have to do that.

Put Recruiters' Minds at Ease

An H-1B visa is fairly simple to file for with proper legal assistance and fairly inexpensive (about $5K or $6K per filing, including government and attorney fees). On the other hand, a permanent-residency application is complex, lengthy, and more expensive ($10K or more), and it does require a company to prove to the U.S. government that no qualified U.S. worker is available to fill the position. Organizations that haven't hired many foreign nationals (international students) may be fearful of the high costs and complexity of filing for a green card, and in many cases this is putting the cart before the horse. Working in H-1B status and proving your worth to the employer is important for future green-card filing.

Some employers may be confused about the differences between an H-1B visa and a green card. If you sense that the employer may be concerned about filing for permanent residency on your behalf, *if* they're thinking that far ahead, it may pay off for you to say the following:

> *I'm thrilled about the opportunity to work for you for a period of seven years—one year of OPT and six years as an H-1B worker—with minimal paperwork and costs. Seven years is a long time. I can make a strong impact in your firm during this period of time. After seven years, we have options as well. If you're satisfied with my performance and wish for me to stay at your firm, we'll have options to explore.*

Between one year of OPT (which is generally how international students start working after graduation) and six years of H-1B (which, at press time, was the maximum amount of time you can hold an H-1B), you could be on payroll for seven years without your firm having to worry about filing for your green card. Seven years is a long time! After six years, your employer could file for your green card, typically the next step down the immigration path, and you could become a permanent resident of the United States. There are options. Note that this chapter does not address the green-card process.

Take the emotion out of the discussion. If the employer believes in you and likes you, then this statement should work—I've seen students have great success with it. You may find some companies that might be willing to provide you with an H-1B visa but might not be willing to file for your permanent residency. But once again, do not bring up any questions regarding permanent residency during the interview process. Don't ask, "Will you be filing for my green card?"

The H-1B Visa and H-1B Transfers: FAQs

The H-1B visa is usually the work visa that international students are looking for. Be very careful about what you read about work visas on the internet. There's much erroneous information out there. Detailed, credible visa information is available on the website of USCIS (www.uscis.gov), the government agency that oversees lawful immigration to the United States.

Following are five FAQs regarding H-1Bs:

1) Does an H-1B petition filed by a small or mid-size company have a greater risk of being rejected?

No. Company size technically doesn't impact your approval chances. An H-1B petition from Microsoft has the same chance of approval as the filing from a 50-person firm that has never sponsored an H-1B worker before. You and your employer must document that the position offered is in a specialty occupation—one that requires a degree—and that the job is tied to your field of study. Again, if a firm is interested in hiring you, they'll probably consult with an attorney to understand the eligibility requirements, etc.

2) I'm currently on an H-1B through company A, but I want to move to company B. Do I need a new H-1B? And when can I start working for company B?

Your existing H-1B will be transferred by filing a new H-1B petition. You may join your new company as soon as the government receives your H-1B visa transfer application from your future employer. *This can be done at any time of the year.* This is a great perk, because it gives you complete freedom to change jobs as an H-1B worker at any time of the year. Just make sure you don't quit your job until you've found another one and your new employer has filed an H-1B petition on your behalf.

Employers *will* want to know how much time you have left on your H-1B. This is key. If you're planning on changing companies, don't waste time: start targeting the firms you want to work for right away. If you have very little time left on your H-1B (less than three years, let's say), employers might be reluctant to consider you unless they plan on filing for your permanent-residency status right away, which may be unlikely. The more time you have on your H-1B, the more attractive you usually are an H-1B transfer employee. Remember that and plan your job changes accordingly! Don't wait too long to act on a job change once you secure your H-1B. You don't have this luxury. Seek advice, be decisive, have a plan, and move fast.

The vastness of the U.S. economy creates all types of opportunities for workers. You are competent, motivated, and in control. If you're not happy with your job, you don't have to stick with it for very long. Changing jobs will not be a black eye on your resume. If an interviewer questions why you want to leave a job you accepted not too long ago, consider a response like this:

> *I accepted my current position in good faith, but I felt that it was a stepping stone toward something more closely aligned with my long-term career goals and passions. The job at your firm is what I've envisioned myself doing right after graduation. I wish we had met sooner.*

Life tends to get much easier once you make the initial transition from being an F-1 student to an H-1B worker. You will be calmer. You will be able to breathe and sleep better at night. Short-term sacrifices may lead to great success long term, including a green card, if that's what you want. Put the right building blocks in place so when the right job opportunity emerges, you're ready.

If you intend to remain in the United States long term, understand this: you are likely to change jobs, careers, industries, and functions several times along the way. You may not keep your first job out of college for very long. There's tremendous mobility in corporate America, and little stigma should you switch career paths, particularly when you can swiftly explain why you made the changes you made. In fact, if you stick with the same job for too long, some people may ask, "What's wrong with you?"

You'll probably come across individuals in the United States who have built incredibly successful careers by changing jobs every four or five years, and even moving from industry to industry. Some people are really good at reinventing themselves, and you will find that U.S. work culture provides motivated individuals with an ongoing sense of renewal about their careers. This type of work culture may not exist where you're from, which is why it's so critical to be self-aware so you can leverage these opportunities and reinvent yourself with confidence. Work is very fluid in the United States, and not long term. In a 2011 longitudinal study of 9,000 men and women born from 1980 to 1984, the U.S. Bureau of Labor Statistics found that about 70% of jobs held by those with a bachelor's degree or higher lasted less than two years.

Stability is dead as well. News about U.S. firms of all sizes laying off workers—sometimes thousands at a time—isn't that noteworthy anymore. Remember Fang Wang? Here is an email she sent me about 17 months after she'd accepted a job that was a great fit for her:

> *Well, life sometimes likes to cast something totally unexpected. I was terminated this morning, without any precursor or anything.*

I got this news as I was finishing the writing *The International Advantage*. At the beginning of my writing process, I'd never suspected that I would be using Fang Wang's story as a way to illustrate my assertion that stability is dead—but here it is.

As an international student, your ability to remain in the United States is often tied to employment after graduation. You have to consider what trends like layoffs may mean to you. The great news is that the vastness of the U.S. economy allows those who work hard and believe in themselves the chance to bounce back. Though I was somewhat shocked when Fang Wang told me she had lost her job, she regrouped mentally and utilized the job-search skills she'd acquired to quickly secure another job.

3) Does the H-1B cap affect the H-1B transfer process?

No, it does not. The H-1B transfer is an entirely different process, and it has nothing to do with the H-1B cap. If there are no more H-1B visas available in a given year and you've already secured one, you have nothing to worry about. You've completed the hardest part of the process. Celebrate that!

4) I'm worried that my current employer will find out about the H-1B transfer. What do I need to tell them?

Relax. You're not obligated to tell your current employer anything, so don't! Your current employer will not know about the transfer. There may be hard feelings at the end when you leave, but it's just business, and these things happen all the time. Do your best to manage this process so you don't burn any bridges. Talk with your career advisor for guidance.

5) Is there any limit on the number of H-1B transfers?

No, there isn't. This is one of the reasons I highly encourage international students to create job-search strategies that take advantage of how friendly the current H-1B transfer regulations are. Your main challenge as a job seeker will be to identify companies that are willing to take you on as an H-1B transfer employee. It will be done on a case-by-case basis, once again. Companies often don't clearly disclose in a job description whether they accept H-1B transfers. You should apply for the job unless the job posting specifically says, "H-1B transfers not accepted."

Don't assume that recruiters and hiring managers are aware of how simple an H-1B transfer can be. In this area, some explaining on your part can make a world of difference. My experience has shown that many companies don't understand the advantages of the H-1B transfer program, and how hassle-free it can be for them.

An Open Door

Given how relatively easy it is to transfer H-1B visas, you may find that some employers who aren't willing to grant you an H-1B visa would be happy to consider you as a candidate on an H-1B visa transfer. Take this excerpt from a job posting as an example:

> *Job Title:*
>
> *Senior Auditors (H-1B Transfers Accepted!)*
>
> *About the Job:*
>
> *Our client, an international public accounting firm, has several available positions in Audit in the Milwaukee area at the Senior level. Successful candidates will lead audit engagements for corporate and governmental clients. Current H-1B visa holders are welcome to apply (i.e., individuals who are already in the United States, have an H-1B visa, and would only need a visa transfer).*

This employer has made it a point to target individuals who already have an H-1B. This employer may not be interested in going through the process of filing an H-1B petition but is happily willing to accept an H-1B transfer.

From a job-search standpoint, some international students might benefit from a strategy that allows them to initially land a position to get their first H-1B where they are mostly competitive, and then create opportunities to move their career in the direction they want. So if your first job out of college does not completely excite you, don't despair. Have a good attitude about it. Improve your base of contacts and your confidence level, and find a way to move your career in the direction you initially envisioned.

When to Bring Up Visas

You finally have a recruiter interested in you. At what point should you bring up visas? Career-center professionals have wrestled with this question at least since I arrived in the United States as an international student back in 1994.

Don't Bring It Up

Most advisors agree that international students should avoid any discussion about sponsorship or work authorization until they're asked about it. The question "Do you sponsor?" can indeed be a showstopper. Asking the question prematurely introduces a barrier to the engagement process, and it can sometimes mean the end of a great conversation between an applicant and a recruiter. The question can prevent international students from building rapport and credibility.

Do Bring It Up (Sometimes)

Some of the students I work with feel that once the interview has progressed to a certain stage, it may be prudent to *proactively* bring up the topic of sponsorship. When things are getting serious with an employer, bringing up the topic of sponsorship does have its benefits. You'll be the one asking questions, which might help you guide the conversation. Bringing up the topic is also a sign of confidence; and people in the United States value direct communication. You don't want to people to think that you're hiding something, or that your immigration status is a bigger "problem" than it actually is. Once you've had the chance to gain your employer's trust and interest and advance in the interview cycle, it may be okay to say:

> *I've been excited about this interview process, and I believe the role we've been talking about is a really good fit. It aligns perfectly with my background and interests. I'd like to count on your support transitioning from a student visa to a work visa. Does your company support this process for the right candidates?*

If you get to the point where a company is ready to fly you out to their headquarters for a final interview round, and you're still unsure if they sponsor or not, consider using the statement above.

The decision to introduce your visa status into a conversation is personal and individual. Try to read the context of the situation you're in before deciding how to proceed. Do some research on the company to understand its sponsorship history. Check www.myvisajobs.com. You may be able to see if employees in your functional area have been sponsored.

Remember: you are not legally obligated to disclose your visa status, so it's ultimately your call.

A Middle-of-the Road Approach

Instead of broaching too much too soon, or too little too late, consider this middle-of-the-road strategy. You might say the following:

> *I've done some research on your firm, and it seems you have a history of sponsoring employees, which speaks in my opinion to the kind of company you are. Is the job I'm applying for a position the company is willing to petition for an H-1B?*

Eight Rules for the Visa Talk

Talking about visas with hiring professionals can be uncomfortable regardless of whether you bring up the subject or they do. Here are some rules you need to follow. They're not difficult to learn, but be sure to practice them with your advisor.

1) Avoid excessive detail.

Excessive detail may give the impression that hiring you will be complicated. Concise answers are key; don't introduce technical information about the H-1B filing process into the conversation. Less is more.

2) Ask politely.

You don't need to convince a company to change their policy for hiring international students. You need to convince them to hire you. At the appropriate moment, say, "I'm currently on a student visa and would need your support to work in the United States after graduation. Do you consider international candidates in certain instances?" This question conveys the type of confidence that many U.S. recruiters are looking for.

3) Don't volunteer to pay for processing fees.

While it is technically not illegal for you to pay certain H-1B filing fees, it is generally not considered good practice. Avoid these scenarios. Many international students believe that companies will be more willing to hire them if they offer to pay the H-1B filing fees. That's normally not the case. A decent employer will cover your H-1B filing costs.

4) Push back (a little).

If you ask the question above and receive "No, we don't sponsor" as the answer, try taking the discussion a bit further if you feel you're a great fit for the role you're interviewing for. A possible follow-up could be:

I understand. Would it be possible for you to investigate if excep-
tions have been made in the past for top candidates? The reason I'm
asking for this favor is because this job is such a good fit for me, and
I really feel I could excel in this role. Any support you could provide
is appreciated.

Put yourself out there. Show how hungry and confident you are. People like that! A confident and serious candidate will try to open a door that was initially closed. The odds may be against you, but you never know until you try. U.S. culture values those who don't give up, who believe in themselves, and who sometimes don't take "no" for an answer. What do you have to lose? Nothing! So give it a try if a) you *really* want the job, b) you believe you're a *really* good fit for the position, and c) you *truly* feel it's a mistake for the company not to hire you.

In this case, you are attempting to convince a hiring manager to check with HR to see if an exception to the H-1B policy could be made. You need advocacy sometimes. In a multicultural global environment where you will be speaking a second language and playing by rules you may not fully understand, this may not be easy, but with a little bit of practice, it can be done. Consider this possible response as well:

I completely understand your position. Many companies seem ap-
prehensive about hiring international students given the current
regulations. An immigration attorney who works with our school
has assured us that visa sponsorship is a manageable process. I'm
happy to connect you with our attorney if you have any questions
in the future.

5) Don't turn your back on opportunity.

I know students who, after being told that a company didn't sponsor, stayed in touch with their contacts there and ended up getting hired.

These stories are not that rare. In theory, you should not be a less attractive candidate to a recruiter because you need sponsorship. A recruiter may choose not to hire you because you need sponsorship, but a good recruiter will evaluate you separately from the fact that you may need a work visa. Always remember to focus first on why employers should hire you. In the end, if you don't get hired, you want that employer to go home feeling like this: "What a shame. This student is ready for this job. I really wish we provided sponsorship."

There's no reason to be nervous when addressing visa questions during a job interview. The question you'll usually get will be, "Are you fully authorized to work permanently in the United States?" Some students believe that questions about sponsorship mean the end of an interview, and they have a hard time recovering. Keep your energy level high. Look the interviewer in the eye and send him or her the message that the process is manageable.

6) Control the conversation.

Do your best to ensure that the recruiter stays focused on your skills, qualifications, and the value you'll bring to the firm. Don't linger on the visa question. If you're speaking with a small or mid-size firm that has never sponsored before, give the interviewer enough information—but not too much—to calm him or her down about the H-1B visa process. Don't launch into a mini-lecture. Simply say this:

> *The process is doable. I'd be happy to connect you with someone from my school who can address any questions you may have. Thousands of international students get H-1B visas every year. This opportunity is open to companies of any size. I will do what I can to help you make this process as simple as possible.*

Your goal is to keep you and your interviewer engaged.

Of course, even if you answer this question in the best manner possible, it certainly does not mean that the company you're talking to will sponsor you. But you want to be able to control what you can control.

7) Don't lie.

Don't ever try to hide the fact that you're an international student or need authorization to work in the United States. If the question about your immigration status comes up, online or in person, answer truthfully.

8) Engage others to address sponsorship questions on your behalf.

Be sure to mention that there are resources available at your university that can help address sponsorship questions a potential employer may have. A university resource can validate what you've said about what it takes to hire you, providing more credibility to your story. Someone from your university might be able to proactively call the employer you're engaged with—my preferred approach—and say the following:

> *I understand you interviewed one of our students and may have some questions about the sponsorship process. We're prepared to help companies address any questions they may have about hiring our international students, particularly if you've never been through the process before. Feel free to contact me.*

I loved receiving calls or emails from employers after this kind of outreach. What generally started as a conversation about visas often turned into a conversation about the student's strengths, motivation to join the firm, and so on. Depending on how you feel your interviews went, work with your career coach to determine if it might be appropriate for him or her to proactively contact an employer who might have sponsorship questions.

Take a look at this sample email:

Dear Mr. (Employer Name),

I hope you are well. I understand that you have recently interviewed (student name). It is my pleasure to provide you with information regarding the process of hiring international students. I'm very familiar with the process – I went through it myself actually – and I can assure you it's not as bad as many people may think. Also, at no cost to you I can easily connect you with an attorney for a conversation about the H-1B visa filing process.

Should you decide to hire Anisha, the process of providing him with an H-1B visa is actually quite simple, particularly now that Anisha has completed his master's degree. There's a separate pool of 20,000 visas that are available only to those who have earned a master's degree or higher from a U.S. institution of higher education. Anisha would qualify to try to secure a visa out of this pool. This is great news for you and for Anisha as well. The next application date for visas is April 1. It is important that you file on this date to avoid possible issues of visas running out. Early preparation is key. Right now it would not cost your company anything to hire Anisha, as he would be using his OPT (Optional Practical Training) to join your firm. This process is 100% hassle-free for you.

Should you decide to move forward with the process of interviewing Anisha, and should you have any questions regarding sponsorship along the way, I just wanted you to know we have the resources to help you address any questions you may have. Please do not hesitate to contact me.

Sincerely,

Marcelo Barros

In the End, It's Just Paperwork

To conclude our discussion of visas, consider the final thoughts in this job posting by a company called Riot Games, for a Director of Marketing (Latin America) position:

> *NOTE: We want you here, so we wanted to make it extra clear that we DON'T require our applicants to have an active US work authorization. At Riot Games we're about great people and solutions, not red tape and bureaucratic barriers. For the right candidate, we'll sponsor and pay for your H-1Bs, O1s and other US work visas. That's just paperwork, and we've got lawyers for that.*

A Recent Look at H-1B Numbers

- For FY 2023, there were 483,927 H-1B applications for an estimated 85,000 visas.

- For FY 2022, there were 308,613 H-1B applications for an estimated 85,000 H-1B visas.

- For FY 2021, there were 190,098 H-1B applications for an estimated 85,000 visas.

As you can see, recently there has been more demand for H-1B workers than available visas. International students who were not lucky enough to receive an H-1B via the lottery most likely had to leave the United States, re-enroll in some sort of academic program and become an international student again, or maybe marry a U.S. citizen in order to stay in the country. Those who worked for global firms with offices outside the United States might have been transferred to a different location, if lucky.

Increase Odds of Selection

Go for a Masters degree. Based on current rules, your odds of securing your H-1B **are higher** if you qualify to compete for the pool of 20,000 H-1B visas only available to those with a U.S. advanced degree (master's degree or higher).

Consider a STEM degree. If you are getting a STEM degree and remain on OPT you should be able to apply for your H-1B three times due to the reasons described in Chapter 3, "It's Pretty Great to Be an International STEM Major". It's even better if you go for a Masters degree or higher STEM degree.

Secure multiple offers from different firms. There is no prohibition on a visa-seeker having multiple valid petitions filed on his or her behalf by different employers for different job offers. For example, if you are a hot software developer who secures job offers from both Microsoft and Amazon, both firms could submit an H-1B petition on your behalf.

Graduate a little early. Work closely with your academic advisor (good planning is key) to see if you can generate a plan to take all of your required classes prior to the start of the H-1B filing season, which normally happens around March or April every year. Even though most U.S. universities don't officially hold graduation ceremonies until the May or June timeframe, that does not stop you from possibly being able to implement this technique.

Start your planning as soon as you begin your last year in college. If determined that you have completed all of the necessary requirements to earn your degree *before* the start of the H-1B filing season, if you receive a job offer early in the fall, for example, and you are to obtain a formal letter from your university indicating that you have completed your degree requirements, the attorney filing your H-1B petition might be able to use this information to apply for your H-1B while you are still in school.

Alternatively, your H-1B petition might be filed based on your under-graduate degree, while you are still finishing your Masters Degree, for example. Discuss these scenarios with your H-1B filing attorney to see if they could apply to you.

Remember this: it is essential for you to obtain OPT. As you enter your last year in college, stay closely in touch with your university International Student Services office, and do not miss important deadlines such as filing for OPT.

13

JOB-SEARCH STRATEGIES YOU MUST USE

You may have heard of a famous tennis player from Spain called Rafael Nadal. Many describe the Spaniard as one of the best tennis players in the history of the sport. Nadal has never been perceived as a hard-court player, though. The ball bounces faster on hard courts—they're made out of concrete—and Nadal's preferred style (his natural strength) has always relied on a slower-bouncing ball. On clay courts, where the ball bounces more slowly compared to hard courts, Nadal feels right at home. For years he was practically unbeatable on clay.

Nadal has had a history of injuries over the years, which isn't unusual for first-class tennis players who push their bodies to the limit, and he now has difficulty running. In order to succeed as a tennis player, one needs to be able to run, correct? Yes, in theory. But if you can't run too well, and if you still want to be the best player in the world, you must compensate. In Nadal's case, compensating means playing with extreme precision. For every move he makes on the court, Nadal has a clear purpose so he can conserve his energy. He needs to be precise. He avoids hitting balls over the net without a clear purpose, much the same way you'll need to be very clear regarding which jobs you should apply for and which ones you shouldn't bother with.

In order to help him, Nadal's coach, who happens to be his uncle, places water bottles on specific parts of the court and tells him, "This is where the ball needs to land. Exactly here. Hit the water bottle." And Nadal practices, practices, and practices some more, and tries to hit the water bottles on the court.

We can all learn several things from Nadal as he hits hundreds of shots in order to achieve the type of precision he needs to win. He practices with deliberation, and he's one of the best in the world. You'll need to do the same as a job seeker: you're going to need to practice a lot in order to win. Nadal does not do it alone. He has a coach who knows just what Nadal needs to do to win. Chapter 1 introduced you to concepts that will help you get the most out of your relationship with your career advisor. He or she will work alongside you to help you achieve your job-search goals.

It won't be easy to get really good at telling people what you can do for them. It won't be easy to summarize your value proposition in a single sentence that gets people excited about wanting to learn more about you.

As graduation approaches, it will be easy to lose balance and find yourself unsure about what type of jobs you should be targeting.

With deliberate practice and good coaching, you can manage the challenges you'll face as an international job seeker and learn how to comfortably share with the world your unique talents.

Think Like Nadal

Even the best athletes in the world encounter environments that don't completely suit them. As a job applicant, you will as well. Nadal feels right at home on clay courts, and not quite at home on hard courts. What kinds of jobs out there make you feel "right at home"? In the end, if you are determined to stay in the United States after graduation, you'll need to create a job-search strategy that enables you to leverage as many of your existing strengths as possible. Sometimes your chances of securing a job offer will greatly depend on whether you can find roles where the fit is undeniable, where you can shine and beat your competition without even trying. For many international students, this means doing something closely related to what they did before. "Wait a minute," you may say. "I came to the United States to move my career in a different direction." Let's hope that happens. It's certainly possible to achieve this goal, but if you and your coach feel you are falling behind, a good plan B is to target roles that closely match your previous educational and professional background.

Finding the Jobs that Fit You

Keep the following suggestions in mind:

1) Assess your chances.

With the help of mentors and your career advisor, determine which roles you're competitive for, and which ones you're not. Apply maximum focus on the positions you're a natural fit for, particularly as graduation is approaching. Nadal doesn't throw the ball over the net without purpose. Similarly, you should not apply for jobs you're not competitive for. Why waste time, effort, and energy pursuing roles you don't have much chance of getting? Frustration is likely if you target the wrong positions and the wrong types of companies. Frustration will lead to discouragement, and discouragement will prevent you from applying energy and focus onto the opportunities you should be targeting. You'll have to conserve emotional energy, because the job-search marathon for international students can be long.

Fang Wang excelled in this strategy. As a busy MBA, she used her time very wisely and avoided applying for roles she wasn't competitive for. Fang's work history consisted of a few part-time jobs that didn't add up to more than two years of work experience. Her resume was not clean. She focused on entry-level MBA jobs and ignored roles that required more than three years of work experience. Her strategy was effective: she was getting bites. Every time I saw her, she'd announce another upcoming interview with a quality firm.

2) Avoid desperate, long-shot applications.

Come graduation, international students who don't have jobs start applying for positions they're not a fit for—and often aren't interested in—simply because the position is open to international students and they're scared of going home. This strategy rarely works. Employers and hiring managers can sense when you're desperate and applying for a position for the wrong reasons. Sometimes staying the course is still your best chance. Your career coach will be able to help you make these kinds of decisions.

3) Remember to compensate.

You may not have all the skills and experiences listed on a job description, but you can still get hired. Nobody is a perfect package. Everyone has limitations. Every recruiter is looking for great communicators who have creative, advanced analytical skills; are tech savvy; are interesting; can inspire others; and can grow into terrific leaders. The perfect hire does not exist. We all have strengths and weaknesses, and smart job seekers compensate. Since Nadal can't run well, he must be smart about how he plays. You must know your weaknesses—as Nadal knows his is running—and work around them, as opposed to trying to correct them. You must be smart about the types of roles and companies you pursue. Chapter 16, "Choosing the Right Targets," presents a methodology that has served MBAs and might also work for job seekers from other disciplines.

Create job-search strategies that focus on what you do best. As discussed previously remember that it is your strengths that will get you hired. Identify companies and jobs where your fit is undeniable. That is certainly one way to succeed.

The Profile of Success

Many international students secure great jobs in the United States. What's the profile of this successful candidate? Career coaches try to look for themes and patterns among successful job seekers so we can share best practices with future students. For someone like me, who is particularly interested in observing how international students adapt to and thrive in the United States, looking for themes that can explain success is an ongoing exercise. I've observed that international students who secure great jobs often have the following characteristics:

- They are good communicators. They're able to interact with faculty, career advisors, recruiters, hiring managers, career coaches, and their American colleagues with ease. They have a sense of openness about them. They are not too shy. Less extroverted people who are more inflexible in their approach may have more difficulty.

- They're not afraid to put their ideas and thoughts forward for consideration even when their language skills are not as strong as they'd like them to be. They don't use language as an excuse not to engage with people. They make an effort to communicate clearly. They don't let their tongue get lazy. They enunciate their words. They may have an accent, but people can easily understand them.

- They are socially savvy. They compliment others. They know that sincere flattery, for instance, goes a long way in the United States.

They monitor social situations skillfully and adjust their behavior appropriately. They have a good understanding of the day-to-day dynamics of life in the United States. They're friendly, and that draws people to them.

- They are always in "learning mode" and are intensely curious about everything that is happening around them. They are not passive observers about the new world they're living in. They make themselves visible and engage.

- Their professional background is not generic. Their resumes are extremely specific and contain key words and experiences recruiters look for. Similarly, they often have sought-after hard skills, such as STEM skills, in fields where there's normally a short supply of domestic candidates. If they're in finance, they may be working toward certifications that will differentiate them in the marketplace. If they're in marketing analytics, at a minimum they know SAS and SQL and other software packages that employers value. Whatever their field, they have a clear understanding of what hiring managers and recruiters are looking for.

- Their soft skills may not be outstanding—sometimes they are average communicators—but they focus on what they do best, compensate, and get hired.

- They sometimes don't have a super high GPA. They do well academically, but they may not be the best students in their class. They focus their time and energy on networking and moving their job-search goals forward.

- They show a tremendous amount of initiative and drive. They don't just rely on on-campus recruiting to succeed. While they closely monitor which companies coming to campus are open to interviewing international students, they are not afraid to network, get off campus (both physically and virtually), and go after the jobs they deserve by talking with people who appreciate their talents and understand their job-search goals.

No international candidate has all of these characteristics. But the more you do have, the easier your job search may be. And here's the great news: every single one of these characteristics can be learned over time, and the frameworks listed on this book help you accomplish these goals.

First Step: Prioritize

When you begin planning your job search, determine your goals, validate your priorities, and assess how much you're willing to compromise. Consider these questions to get the ball rolling:

- Are you flexible about job title, level of responsibility, industry, and pay? Which of these variables are you willing to compromise on? Getting to your dream job is a journey. You may not be totally satisfied with your first job out of school. But if you're moving your career in the right direction, you may just find yourself in your dream position down the road. Your plan B job sometimes ends up working out very well. It is particularly important for international students to understand the need to compromise and to be competitive when applying for jobs.

- How do you feel about working for a quality mid-size firm that no one has heard of but wants to hire you and give you an H-1B visa?

- Are you willing to be the very first H-1B worker a company has ever had?

- How about working in the United States for one year and then returning home after OPT is over? Are you comfortable with this scenario?

- Would you consider some sort of international rotational program that may have you living in different countries and perhaps attempt a transfer to the United States later on an L-1[1] visa?

If you don't get your priorities straight, you'll have trouble organizing your job search.

Focus on Your Strengths

You already know that savvy job seekers know they'll be most successful when they focus on their strengths, rather than try to rectify their weaknesses. This notion is even more important for international students. There are at least two challenges. First, there may be a lack of awareness around who you are and what you do well. Are you aware of the distinct strengths that will help you be a more successful job seeker? Become critically aware of all the life experiences you've had that may have shaped who you are as a person. This cultural and personal awareness will be key to the success of your job search.

Acknowledging your strengths and talking about them with confidence can be painful for international students who have been raised to downplay/understate their talents and achievements, but who now find themselves in the land of self-promotion, where they regularly hear people talking about how great they are. When I ask international students to list their strengths, their responses are often vague. Some are paralyzed

---

[1] An L1 visa allows U.S companies that have branches outside of the U.S. to transfer certain classes of employee from its foreign operations to the USA. Some U.S firms that rarely use the H-1B visa program are extensive users of the L1 visa program.

by the question. Many have never taken the time to think through what they do well. If they have, they are not able to say it.

International students need to see, accept, and appreciate their strengths in order to increase their motivation, confidence, and overall job-search success. Introspection and a close partnership with your career advisor can help you recognize talents you may have had all along but that your culture may have prevented you from recognizing. International students often have a great deal of "raw intelligence"—they're smart and do well academically—but often lack an understanding of how to convert intelligence into skills and value that get them hired.

Developing specific language that helps you speak about your strengths and successes in a manner you're comfortable with can be helpful. Try completing the following statements:

> *Since arriving in the United States, I've noticed that . . . .*
>
> *My friends/professors have told me that doing . . . . . . comes naturally to me.*
>
> *I have received positive feedback regarding my ability to . . . .*

It will not be sufficient to tell great stories to U.S. recruiters and hiring managers. You will have to ground your job-search campaign on traits, skills, and strengths that match as much as possible what the employer is looking for.

Leveraging Newly Discovered Skills

Many international students discover new passions and skills during their studies. In some cases, you may have had the talents you think you developed in the United States all along. The new context of living overseas has helped you see something you do well. Maybe no one at home validated that you were great at something, but when you arrived in the United States, that changed. "I didn't know I was so good at math until I came to the United States," a first-year MBA from South Korea once told me. In South Korea, surrounded by friends and classmates who performed as well or better than he did, Jihoon never considered himself good at math. But in the United States, he found himself standing out, excelling, and enjoying quantitative classes more than ever. Jihoon had been repeatedly told he had a "gift for manipulating numbers" by his U.S. classmates, something he had never heard before in his life. How you feel about your newfound strengths as an international student will be key in determining the types of jobs you may want to seek, and your motivation for pursuing them. Jihoon fully capitalized on a strength he hadn't known he possessed and aggressively pursued jobs that took advantage of his aptitude for managing numbers.

Select a Niche Market

To select a niche market, you should focus on targeting jobs where you have a competitive advantage. It can be a skill, work experience, or knowledge that is unique or rare and cannot be easily duplicated by your competition. Maybe you know a lot about molecular biology or you have advanced programming skills that allow you to effortlessly create bug-free apps. Maybe you have an eye for spotting discrepancies on financial statements. Whatever it is, be extremely specific.

As discussed in Chapter 3, "It's Pretty Great to Be an International STEM Major," one way to increase your chances of obtaining employment in the United States is to have skills and work experience that other applicants don't have. At the MBA level, some students have secured great jobs in technology consulting because, in general, there's a shortage of qualified domestic workers with "techie" skills. Generalists are abundant, and you don't want to come across as one of them. Be very specific when speaking about your skills and the impact you can have, and remember that STEM skills are in demand.

Avoid broad, idealistic generalizations like, "I'd like to get a job in finance."

Don't Be Afraid to Change Your Job-Search Strategy (But Do It Wisely)

Some international students insist on sticking to their original job-search plan because they feel persistence will pay off. This approach can be highly detrimental to your success. As graduation quickly approaches and the possibility of going home becomes more of a reality, only at this point, out of desperation, do they try something they haven't tried before.

Don't wait too long to widen your job-search targets or change your job-search direction entirely. You may have to expand your industry, functional area, or geographical location. You have a limited window of opportunity to shift gears during your studies; you'll need to allow enough time to uncover positions you're competitive for. Sometimes international students wait too long to change tactics. If you are constantly engaged with your career coach, then you don't have to worry about when to change gears.

Continue to revise and fine-tune your job. Consider this scenario:

Yang was targeting the big-name consulting firms as a second-year MBA. But with the arrival of the second half of her second year as an MBA and no consulting interviews in sight, she was falling behind. Due to no particular fault of her own, she was just not gaining momentum in a space that is extremely competitive. Not wanting to go home, she needed a correction and a new strategy if she were to have a chance to stay in the United States after graduation. It was time for her to focus on her plan B and target roles that more closely matched her pre-MBA work experience. Prior to Business school Yang had worked at KPMG as a Supervising Senior, Global Transfer Pricing Service, for about 3 years. Her plan B strategy was to focus on roles that closely matched what she had done previously. In the end she succeed and secured a quality job as a Senior Transfer Pricing Analyst at CNH Industrial.

By shifting gears, Yang improved her chance of success. Perhaps what brought you to the United States was the prospect of an exciting career change; if that doesn't work, falling back on what you did previously may be your best bet. Yang did not recalibrate on her own. The going-forward strategy was to focus on jobs where her fit was undeniable. This can be a successful strategy, but remember that for some international students, it may mean you'll end up in a job very similar to what you did before you came to the United States.

When you feel unsure about what to do next, particularly when rejections are coming in, consult with a career advisor. Even if you feel certain what your next move might be, validating your idea with your career advisor is a great habit and an excellent way for you to enhance your working relationship with him or her. If you have been receiving good feedback from recruiters, alumni, and mentors, then it may make sense to stick with the "original game plan" you have in place. But if you've sent out a ton of resumes and networked with the right people and *still* find that nothing is happening, you have to assess what's going on. If you're falling behind, something about you or your job-search approach probably should be corrected. Identifying what this is on your own is hard. Talk to your career coach.

Job-Winning Strategies

Below are some tips on how to increase your chances of successfully gaining employment in the United States. Some of these have been mentioned before but are worth repeating.

1) Know yourself.

Forget about visas and sponsorship challenges for a minute. Who are you and what do you love? *Always* start your job search with your interests and passions, not with a list of companies that may be open to sponsoring.

2) Benchmark yourself against everybody out there.

Your skill set and career aspirations are probably not that unique. Base your job-search strategy on what has worked—and hasn't worked—for other students with similar profiles and career aspirations. Compare your profile to that of those who seek the same type of role you're targeting. Seek to learn from and partner with others, not compete.

3) Learn about failures, not just successes.

Every school has examples of international students who did not get jobs in the United States, but their stories aren't posted on your school's website or included on job-search panels your career center organizes. Success stories get promoted, but you may glean even more value by learning from students who felt they did not achieve their job-search goals. Ask your career advisor to put you in touch with international students who focused on the same types of jobs you're interested in but who did not secure work in the United States after graduation. Reach out to them for a candid conversation about their job-search struggles, and ask these questions:

- What do you think prevented you from finding a job in the United States?

- Do you think you could you have managed your job search differently, or were there simply factors outside of your control that prevented you from receiving a job offer?

- What advice do you have for me as someone who wants to stay in the U.S after graduation?

4) Gather input from everyone you know.

Learn as much as you can from others but realize that you're a unique individual who will have to generate a job-search strategy that fits you. Don't make important decisions on your own. There's no need to do so.

5) Utilize social media.

By using common social-media tools, you can keep in touch with international students from other universities to find out how their job search is going. A company that sponsors may not come to your school, but if you're in touch with other students, you may be able to easily identify companies that sponsor that could be recruiting at a school nearby. You may be able to leverage resources and events that are open to students from other universities. Find out if other schools' career advisors recommend different job-search strategies than those recommended by your advisor. Be smart. Learn. Make new friends. Stay connected with international students from other schools. Career fairs like Black MBA and NSHMBA are great places to connect with other international students.

6) Don't believe everything you hear.

Smart people consult with accountants before making huge financial investments. They speak with doctors before taking a medicine for some discomfort they may be having. Value your mentors and career coaches —those who have your best interests in mind and the training and experience to help you—and avoid making critical job-search decisions on your own. There are many myths out there regarding how international students can find an H-1B job, for example. Similarly, be wary of paid Internet services that promise you the H-1B job of your dreams. When in doubt, consult with your career advisor.

7) <u>Get in front of the right people.</u>

As much as your career coach is a great ally in your quest to get a job, he or she may not have the right set of professional experiences to fully appreciate your talents, and give you full credit for what you may have accomplished professionally. Whatever field you're interested in, you will need to interface with those who can readily "see" your talents and give you the credit you deserve. Connect with people in your field of interest, particularly those who understand your skill set. Join industry or trade associations in the fields you are targeting and talk to people who get you.

8) <u>Choose partners wisely.</u>

Stay away from individuals whose agendas seem to be to manage your expectations—to tell you only how hard it's going to be—rather than help you generate plans and strategies to help you get closer to achieving your goals. Partner with those who believe in you and want you to secure a great H-1B job. Some people can make you feel energized. Others make you feel tired. Treasure your relationships with those who believe in you. Thank these individuals often for their support.

9) <u>Be flexible.</u>

International students may need to expand their job search by considering jobs outside their desired career and functional area. For example, a Computer Science major who'd like to do web development may also want to search for jobs in other areas of IT. Depending on your skill set, career goals, and interests, you could develop multiple positioning statements that would change depending on your audience.

10) <u>Live a balanced life.</u>

Completely forget about your job search sometimes, and make time for fun in your new culture. Create a well-balanced stay for yourself in the

United States. Travel. Visit a museum. Learn a new sport. Do something you would not normally do. Get out of our comfort zone. When not studying or working, what do you do for fun? A well-rounded experience in the United States will make you a more interesting, calm, and successful job seeker.

A Final Strategy: Work for Free

Many undergraduate international students never worked in high school or college before going abroad. They were given a clear mission of working hard in school, getting good grades, not getting in trouble, and not worrying about work until after graduation. Making the switch to get into a "work mindset" is not automatic. If you want to try to stay in the United States after graduation, you will be much more competitive if you work during your studies. This idea goes beyond simply competing for paid internships. If you have limited work experience and want to become more marketable, then look for ways to work for free a few hours a week. Always check with your university before accepting non-paid employment to see if you are able to work. Unpaid internships can be a great start.

Maybe you're getting an accounting degree and can help a small CPA firm process some tax forms during a busy time of year. Invest in your future and add U.S. work experience to your resume. U.S. work experience will be easier for employers to verify as well.

If you find yourself without a job after graduation and still want to stay in the United States, utilize your OPT toward some sort of temporary work engagement. This is an unpopular option for some international students, who feel they're "wasting" their OPT. However, this really isn't a waste, particularly if you don't have a full-time job offer. You can continue your job search while you hold some sort of temp work. And you never know: unpaid internships have converted into H-1B jobs. I know someone who worked as an unpaid intern at a nonprofit organization in Washington, DC, called the Brazilian Industry Coalition (BIC) who is now a full-time employee at the same organization, with an H-1B visa in her hand. This is what Gracielle Palma, Manager at Brazil Industries Coalition, had to share with international students looking for a job:

> *My advice for international students who are looking for an H-1B job is to consider all options and to find organizations that fully leverage their backgrounds. Don't be discouraged by unpaid internships. Work hard, do a good job, network, and you will get noticed. When I started at BIC I did had no idea that I would eventually become a paid full-time employee at the organization with my H-1B visa.*

Because you have developed a strong list of contacts throughout your stay in the United States, you can now contact people in your network and propose a short-term "consulting" engagement. Don't ask for a job. Instead, present a vision and a project scope with deliverables. Everyone is looking for good help. Consider this sample:

> *I realize that your firm is expanding rapidly in Southeast Asia, and I feel I have some unique insight on how distributors work in that part of the world. I would like to propose a project where I can help you assess the current caliber of your channels and create ways to help them be more effective. I have developed a proposal for you to consider. I am currently looking for a short-term consulting engagement and would be delighted to help you and your team reach your goals.*

Work with the right resources at your university to understand what employment options might be available before you reach out to prospective employers. Always check with your university before you accept any type of employment in the United States, either paid or unpaid. Once you're clear on the options, contact people who could profit from your skills and talents. Introduce who you are, and offer help. Everyone is looking for good help.

14

THE CHAPTER YOU DON'T WANT TO READ: RETURNING HOME AFTER GRADUATION

This purpose of this chapter is to shed light on a recent type of recruiting activity that directly impacts international students, particularly students from large populous countries such as India and China, for example.

Enticing to Employers—and Still Enrolled in School

For most multinationals, hiring is still a "local" activity. That means Microsoft China handles their hiring needs locally out of their China office, and the same is mostly true for other large multinationals. However, depending on where you're from, you may be affected by a new trend: some well-known global employers might try to hire you while you're still pursuing your degree in the United States. Some employers aren't waiting for you to return home before they hire you. Why risk losing you to a competitor when they can hire you while you're still in the United States, completing your degree?

Grand Promises

Whether the idea appeals to you or not, some large, well-known global firms may *encourage* you to consider working for them in your home country.

You may be courted to consider returning home after graduation to help U.S. firms gain market share and grow their business in your home country.

Recruiters may say, "Why stay in the United States when things are sluggish?" They may even tell you that your career at home may progress faster than if you stay in the United States. And that is true.

You already know that if you go home you'll be a bilingual hire with a degree from a university, and with knowledge of U.S. management competencies. In a 2011 online article published by McKinsey & Company, the CEO of Manpower, a leading global provider of employment services, argues that "any multinational that really wants to grow in emerging markets should think hard about implementing a reverse-expat strategy of its own." The title of his article speaks for itself: "Beyond expats: Better managers for emerging markets." The status of business professionals in high-growth countries around the world has been elevated, and now these individuals are shaping the strategy of the firms they represent.

Not Sold?

I'm not surprised if none of this seems enticing. The option of returning home may not excite you. Resumes from international MBAs indicate that many were already working at big-name firms—sometimes American firms—in their home country before coming to the United States to pursue a graduate degree. So returning home, even at a higher-level position, makes it seem like they haven't advanced their career. A student from China who was getting an MS degree in finance once told me, "If I go back home, it's like I failed."

Try to adjust your thinking. As U.S. organizations face the ongoing pressure to grow, they'll be forced to look for new markets in which to sell their services and products. This trend could, in theory, present international MBAs with terrific opportunities, particularly those who come from an emerging country. If you come from a BRIC nation, you know firsthand how much the world has changed and that there are exciting and profitable job opportunities available to you that were not available to your parents. International students with the know-how to help U.S. firms address the complexities and opportunities of gaining market share on a global scale will be the types of managers and leaders whom companies need to hire. As an international MBA, you might be able to successfully address mergers and acquisitions and do valuations that take into account factors that at times are known only to insiders.

Given the economic growth of countries such as India and China, many companies will now target international students while they're still in the United States. If you're getting an MBA, your degree will be highly attractive. "USA MBA Jobs Visa Hurdles," a 2011 article published by QS Top MBA, an online publication focused on the needs of MBAs around the world, stated the following:

> *"With an increased need for managers with global outlook and mobility, as well as ambitious growth objectives in emerging markets, American employers are finding U.S.-educated foreign nationals an excellent solution to leadership gaps in their offices around the world."*

In the same article, Jeanie Mabie, global employer branding and university recruitment leader at IBM, said:

"We want people with a global mindset. We need to fuel growth in particular countries and that requires strong talent that is geographically mobile."

Going home does not mean you failed. That's certainly not what it meant for a former student of mine named Tiffany from Taiwan, who secured a quality job at HP in her home country. Tiffany's goal was to remain in the United States, but when I asked her how she was feeling, she said, "It's nice to be close to family, and I learned so much about myself." Tiffany went home as a more self-aware individual who didn't let the outcome of her job search determine the quality of her stay in the United States. The value of her study-abroad experience was reflected not just in terms of where she found a job. She was also able to redefine what success meant on her own terms. Her career is just starting. She is working for a great company, and she will have opportunities to move around the world if she chooses to do so. Who knows where life will take her next?

Sell Global Mobility

Are you willing to pack your bags and go places? If so, excellent, because that might make you an attractive candidate for top firms around the world. Consider whether you're ready to position yourself as a candidate who embraces global mobility and expresses willingness to work in various regions of the world. A big-name U.S. organization that might not be able to hire you locally because of visa restrictions might be able to refer you to their international counterpart in a country that has more friendly immigration rules and where your talents are needed. Adopting a job-search strategy of global mobility, especially when targeting large corporations, can improve your chances of success.

You never know where life will take you. If you have a sense of adventure and can't shake an attraction to the gypsy lifestyle, you may want to continue seeing the world after graduation by exploring challenging assignments overseas, beyond the United States. Being close to where the action is at any point in one's career may not only help advance professional growth but also provide wonderful opportunities for personal growth.

A Bold Move for Bold Workers

I was working for Cisco Technologies when CEO John Chambers announced one of his boldest moves: he wanted 20% of senior managers to be working at a globalization center in Bangalore, India, by 2010. He tapped his most trusted top executives to leave Silicon Valley and move to Bangalore. Chambers wanted high-ranking employees to gain critical insight into one of the world's fastest-growing economies. Those who may not be too comfortable yet with the idea of living in a developing country should change this mindset. The shift in mobility will benefit global workers with the kind of know-how and characteristics international students have.

The three stories that follow are from international MBAs I had a chance to work closely with. They went where their talents were most needed and looked at the world as a playground. Each of these students interpreted what it means to be an international student in a slightly different way.

Gain U.S. Experience First (Ryoko's Story)
Ryoko from Japan came into my office one day and said, "Job searching as an international student is

fucking hard, Marcelo." Ryoko's eight years in the United States prior to starting her MBA had given her the chance to quite nicely master U.S. communication style.

Not much about Ryoko was international other than the fact that she had an F-1 visa. Loud and confident, she was popular among her peers, and her resume contained credible work experience, such as working as an auditor for Deloitte. Her skill set was very versatile, and I could see her moving in many different directions. I had confidently placed her in my "will get a great H-1B job" bucket. Ryoko thought she could beat the odds as well.

However, despite her strong credentials, in many ways she faced the same challenges as other international students. She did not get immediately frustrated with the sponsorship barriers she faced; she knew those were common. What Ryoko didn't know when she started her MBA was that her open mind and adventurous spirit would move her life and career in a direction she hadn't envisioned at all. Frequent meetings with Ryoko during the academic year indicated to me that she was willing to explore. She seemed to view the world as a playground, full of opportunities—some she hadn't found yet but knew were out there. Then, one day, through one of those typical MBA asset management clubs where finance students pick stocks and hope for great returns, she discovered a firm that really caught her attention.

Ryoko valued global leadership. She used this term frequently whenever we met. She thought that if a company valued global leadership, then it should be looking for future global leaders, and she was very global. Ryoko came to believe that being international was an advantage in that regard, even though her immigration status prevented her from applying for jobs at many interesting companies. She took every interview invitation seriously and prepared as well as she possibly could.

Covidien seemed to be the right place for Ryoko. "It felt right," she told me. When an offer came in from Covidien's Tokyo office, Ryoko was certain that this was the right move for her. She wanted to return to Japan, but not right away. She describes her experience:

After receiving several offers from employers from different industries, I had the power to negotiate with Covidien. I was invited to Covidien headquarters to do the interview, and I told them I would like to start learning the "corporate culture" at Covidien's headquarters before I started a full-time position in Tokyo. Even though my full-time offer was from the Tokyo office, I emphasized that I could best serve the Tokyo office if I understood the corporate culture. I realized that there were many employees in the Tokyo office who could communicate and write in English, but only a few had "global leader quality." So I immediately negotiated that I would be a much better asset for the Tokyo office after starting in the U.S. office.

So Ryoko negotiated with her firm to spend her OPT time at Covidien's HQ in Minneapolis, Minnesota, before moving permanently to Japan to continue her career. It was a win-win proposal. The idea came from her.

I asked Ryoko for her best tip for international stu-

dents seeking a job. She said, "Tell students to understand the true meaning of globalization." Ryoko,
from Japan, had a very progressive outlook about
what it means to be an international student. Her
mindset is more of an exception than the rule. She
was older and in some ways more mature than other
students in her class. Maybe she had had her "U.S.
fix." Everybody is different.

An Appealing Option for Multinationals

Some global multinationals may be more willing to host MBAs working in the United States for one year, as Covidien did for Ryoko, for
on-the-job training, before sending them home to help their companies capitalize on the growth of certain regions. Companies like this
approach because they don't have to sponsor international students—
they take advantage of OPT to get students on payroll—and therefore
avoid any perceived hassles associated with sponsorship.

Such opportunities allow international students to gain some U.S. work
experience (not to mention a U.S. salary to help with student loans) and
then plan for a smooth transition to their home country after completing
the U.S. assignment.

Following are two excerpts of job postings seeking candidates for this
type of arrangement.

Example #1: Walmart

POSITION TITLE: International Academy
LOCATION: Bentonville, Arkansas, to International Location

FUNCTIONS: Merchandising, Supply Chain and Real Estate

The time spent training in the United States will provide you with the knowledge and training necessary for you to excel in our international locations. Your understanding and execution of the Walmart business model will further increase our success and brand globally.

Qualifications:
Masters or Bachelors degree, preferably from the school of business
Citizen of China, India, or Brazil
Ability to obtain and maintain valid status and employment authorization in your home country during the second phase of the program
Eligible for one year of work in the United States through the OPT portion of your student visa
Fluency in English
High level of adaptability

Upon successful completion of the training program in the United States, the participants will return to their country of origin to work for Walmart.

Example #2: INVISTA

POSITION TITLE: Corporate Development Analyst—Bilingual (Chinese /English)
LOCATION: Kennesaw, Georgia, and Shanghai, China

ABOUT THE JOB: We invite you to consider INVISTA's Back to Asia™ program, which provides high-potential individuals with an understanding of our global businesses. We are currently seeking candidates who are proficient in Mandarin and English to fill roles in INVISTA's Commercial Development capability for our Performance Surfaces and Materials business. **This job will be based in Kennesaw, Georgia, for the first year, and will prepare you for potential relocation to Shanghai, China, after about one year from date of hire. Visas or work permits are not offered; however, moving assistance will be considered for the relocation to Shanghai, China.**

Education, Experience and Skills Required:
Proficiency in Mandarin and English, both written and verbal

Ability to provide original documents which verify your identity and legally authorized right to work in China as part of INVISTA's Back to Asia™ program

Ability to provide Employee Authorization Documentation or otherwise have the ability to work in the United States for approximately one year (this means OPT)

Take the Initiative

If you find a company that has operations in your own country and maybe a branch there, you may want to consider proactively approaching them with an offer to keep you in the United States for 12 months (during OPT) and then transition you to your home country after you complete some formal training at headquarters. In other words, even if you don't see a formal job posting like Walmart's or INVISTA's, don't hesitate to propose something to an employer you're interested in that benefits you and the company. Use a statement like this:

> *Hi. I am very interested in your firm and believe I can help you with your growth plans. I'd like to propose a model where I work for your firm for one year here in the United States after graduation before I get transferred to my home country. Can we please discuss how we might be able to set up such an arrangement? I believe this could work very well and prepare me to hit the ground running upon my return home.*

Below are a couple of examples of two international students who were rather adventurous.

The Third-Country Option (Chih-ming's Story)

Chih-ming worked hard to identify positions in the United States that he was a fit for while also focusing on identifying opportunities outside of the United States that intrigued him. Unlike Ryoko, whose interest in exploring global opportunities arose gradually, Chih-ming focused on trying to find quality job leads in the United States and overseas from day one. Originally from Taiwan, he thought that a cool and challenging job somewhere in Southeast Asia would fit the bill.

Chih-ming might have worked harder as an international job seeker than anyone from his graduating class; he essentially managed a U.S. job search while *simultaneously* scouting for interesting opportunities overseas. That's a lot of work. On top of all that, he still found time to regularly ask me, "Is there anything you need, Marcelo?" He was that kind of person.

In the end, Chih-ming did not blink when the right opportunity appeared for him to apply for a job in Singapore, and that's where life took him. Today, Chih-ming travels throughout Asia as a business development manager representing an architecture firm headquartered in Singapore that has an international clientele. He has a fast-paced lifestyle in a very cosmopolitan city. And when he gets homesick, Taiwan is not too far away. For now, he appears happy and fulfilled. With his sense of adventure, who knows where life will take him next?

Hopping Around the World As a Global Worker (Kemi's Story)

In many ways, Kemi had a sense of adventure similar to Chih-ming's. A chemical engineering gradu-

ate from Nigeria with a data-driven mindset, Kemi
fell in love with supply chain. She found it exciting
to help companies make things faster, cheaper, and
more efficiently by revamping manufacturing processes through voracious data tracking and analysis.

A referral from one of her MBA professors eventually
got Kemi talking with a firm called Hilti. Hilti, a solution provider for the construction industry, makes
tools for construction professionals and has employees in more than 120 countries. It had never crossed
Kemi's mind that the construction industry might be
an exciting place for her.

Sometimes blind dates do work. Kemi and Hilti spoke
a few times and decided to say "yes" to each other.
It seemed like a good match. When I asked Kemi
where she'd be located, she said she'd be spending
her OPT time at the company's U.S. headquarters,
and then she'd be sent somewhere. "Somewhere?"
I asked. "You don't know where you could be going?"
"I don't," she said. "It will depend on the needs of
the business."

In the end, the needs of the business called for
Kemi's talents to be utilized in Saudi Arabia, and
there she went. "I want to see the world while I can,"
she told me. "Let me get out there while I'm single
and have no kids."

If you want to call yourself a global worker, embrace mobility in different
phases of your career, go where the action and innovation are, and have
fun along the way. You could even end up back in the United States,
where your international adventure started, if that's what you wish. Who

knows?

A 2011 PricewaterhouseCoopers (PwC) survey called "Millennials at work: Reshaping the Workplace" found that 71% of Generation Y workers expect and want to complete an overseas assignment during their career. Young Americans seem to recognize the opportunities presented by traveling and working abroad, and this mindset will only benefit international students. It makes sense to get out there to understand this crazy, tiny world we live in. The individuals who seek out these experiences will create enormous professional advantages for themselves, not to mention opportunities for personal growth.

An article published on April 28, 2015 by at Harvard Business Review titled *New MBAs Should Start Their Careers in Frontier Markets* urges MBA graduates to be adventurous and start their career in frontier markets. Author Jonathan Berman, who has experience advising companies that want to enter emerging and frontier markets, states that "spending time early in your career in a frontier market has a lasting impact on all your subsequent management decisions." Many international MBAs have had the luxury of growing up and working in emerging countries before coming to the U.S. If you are from a BRIC country you have observed much transformation and growth recently in the part of the world you are from. What will do you with all of this knowledge? U.S firms are interested in what you have learned. Your awareness about the world sets you apart from MBA graduates who only know one reality, but only if you embrace what you know and have the courage to show others how critical it is to be global. This is not just talk: you need to capitalize on this key strength and position yourself as a professional who will not make decisions in a vacuum, is naturally in tune with the dynamics of the a globalized economy, and recognizes best practices your country may be known for and that U.S firms could learn from.

Negotiating for U.S. Salary Equivalents

Student loan repayment can be a real financial challenge for some international students. Going back home may seem financially impossible. Global employers know that salaries for MBAs in the United States are still considerably higher than in many parts of the world.

Consider the following statement when negotiating with employers for possible jobs outside of the United States:

> *I'm thrilled to have received this offer. Thank you. This job is a great fit for me. I'm concerned, however, about my ability to pay for my student loans—which are in U.S. dollars. Is there anything you might be able to offer me in terms of a signing bonus or something along these lines that might help me address my student-loan obligations? I really feel this is a great opportunity for me, but I am worried about my finances.*

Use this legitimate concern as part of your negotiations with a U.S. company that offers you a job in your home country, particularly if you're still pursuing your studies in the United States. Negotiations should wait until you have an offer in hand and should be based on your ability to add value to an employer, and how unique your background and skill set might be.

It's not unusual for large U.S. multinationals to offer a bonus, housing allowance, or other incentives to help ease international student-loan burdens. Work with your advisor to see if you can come up with effective negotiation strategies. Anything is possible!

Intra-Company Transfers

Starting your post graduation career at home with a large, well-established, global multinational is not what most international MBAs want, in my experience. However, many U.S. multinationals believe in intra-company international employee transfers and leverage the L-1 visa to move someone from their office in Shanghai, for example, to their office in New York City. If you speak English well, understand U.S. customs and business dynamics, and maintain a strong network in the United States, starting your career at home, where you might be highly marketable, may be a smart move. Returning later to the United States after you obtain more work experience is a real possibility.

Find out if the company you're interested in uses intra-company transfers as a talent management tool. You may want to ask, "What opportunities do employees have to move around the world?"

It's not unusual to meet international individuals who live and work in the United States, many of them U.S. citizens, who first entered the United States on an L-1 visa. Many of these professionals were never international students themselves. Their ability to generate value for their firms created exciting global career opportunities. There are many ways to create an exciting global career, if that's what you seek. There are no limits on the number of L-1 visas available, and companies can file for an L-1 visa at any time of the year. These are huge benefits for firms, compared to the constraints of the H-1B program.

If you end up with a job in the U.S. that connects you back to your home country or region, if you don't get lucky with the H-1B lottery and must leave the U.S. at the end of OPT, depending on the needs of your employer, you may be able to work out of the "region" you support and then try to return to the U.S. at a later time, sometimes utilizing an L1 visa, for example.

Whether planned or not, if your first job as an international student ends up being "at home" or elsewhere do not look at this event with disappointment. There are real advantages associated with this approach and there are certainly options available for you to explore that could lead to job assignments in different countries, and a possible transfer to the U.S. later on in your career if that is what you wish. Target U.S multinationals that may have processes in place that support the movement of employees around the world.

15

CONSIDERATIONS FOR INTERNATIONAL MBAS

This chapter lays a basic foundation meant to help international MBAs run the job-search marathon with more confidence. It also highlights key areas that are of interest for international students from any major and some common pitfalls to avoid. So, regardless of what you're studying, read on.

The race for a great H-1B job seems to start the moment MBA students set foot on campus, if not sooner. If admitted into a program, some international MBAs are contacted by their school while they're still at home. The pace of the MBA job-search marathon is fast, but international runners must still remember it is a long-distance race.

But before we move forward, let's review some basic information regarding how international MBAs are faring these days with regards to finding employment in the United States.

MBA Job Reporting for International Students

Current job reporting guidelines don't require universities to report what percentage of international MBAs found jobs in the United States versus how many found a job in their home country or somewhere else outside of the United States. Some universities list the names of companies that have hired international students in the past, but sometimes they don't specify whether an international student was hired by IBM to work in Mumbai, Shanghai, or NYC. Prospective international students should contact current international students in the MBA programs they're considering in order to get the true scoop on a school's track record of placing international students in the United States.

Those who work with international students know firsthand that it can take longer for international students to find jobs. If you are already in business school, you may know this to be true: you see your U.S. classmates landing interviews, while you may be struggling to catch recruiters' interest. You may "win" the job-search marathon toward the end of your studies; it's not unusual for some international MBAs to find employment close to or after graduation, after their American colleagues have secured employment. The journey will be a little different for everyone, of course. Regardless, in order to succeed, MBAs must carefully manage every stage of the job-search process, particularly recently as the resistance to consider international MBAs as hires has generally increased.

Despite the difficulties and the slower job-placement pace, it is certainly possible to be successful and secure a great H-1B job in the United States as an MBA. In fact, some MBA programs informally report that their U.S. job placement rate for international MBAs is on par with that of domestic students.

The Value of an MBA

Congratulations on getting an MBA—but keep this in mind: you don't need the degree to secure a great job in the United States or to be successful in business. Bill Gates, Mark Zuckerberg, and Steve Jobs are the college dropouts everyone knows about, but there are also many other individuals out there—regular people like you and me—who don't have an MBA yet have successful, lucrative, and fulfilling careers in business. Many international MBAs end up with quality jobs in the United States after graduation but not necessarily because they earned an MBA. This is an important realization for international students, as many believe that their MBA is the ticket to a great job with a well-known firm. When international MBAs first arrive in the United States, they sometimes naively think that recruiters will focus on their future career goals. Newly arrived international students are often surprised by how much focus recruiters place on their pre-MBA work history and existing skills.

If you're getting an MBA from a top business school, that's excellent news, because many top U.S. employers that do sponsor tend to target these schools. If you're not attending a top-tier business school but still dream of getting a job with a top-tier firm like Google or Microsoft, don't despair. Top MBA employers in the United States do realize that there's exceptional talent everywhere. Amazon was starting to pay more attention to the MBA students at our program, for example, but we were not part of their list of core schools. Bain & Company has made it clear in several interviews that there is exceptional talent everywhere, not just in the top 10 MBA programs, and part of their job is to find it. There are great opportunities for everyone. Some MBAs will have to work much harder than others to accomplish their job search goals and secure a job in the U.S. after graduation.

Coupled with the right type of professional experience, the MBA degree can be a wonderful excuse for international students to connect and get noticed by top employers in the United States.

Top Job-Searching Tips for MBAs

All of the previous topics covered in this book apply to MBAs. In the spirit of emphasizing what is most important for MBAs, let's review some key strategies here.

Define Your Interests

Fashion. Finance. Supply chain. Sports. Video games. Data modeling. Big firms. Start-ups. Knowing what you like is key, truly the foundation of a successful job search. You won't get a job at Microsoft unless you appreciate and get excited about technology. Besides one-on-one career counseling, take the career assessments provided by your career center seriously; some of them are specially designed for business students. Remember, however, that these assessments do not take into account cultural differences that may change how you interpret the results.

Move Fast but Not Too Fast

It's true that the earlier you identify your interests and the type of work you're seeking, the more time you have to uncover suitable job leads. There is value in moving a bit more slowly than your peers, however. An international student from China told me she was certain she wanted to focus on finance because she took the time to explore and learn about fields that, in the end, she knew were not for her. When she made her choice, she did it with confidence, even though it took her a bit longer than her classmates to decide what she wanted to focus on.

Recognize the Fluid Boundaries Between Functional Areas

Understanding who you are, what you like to do, and where you best fit is far more important than agonizing about which functional area is right for you.

Yes, you will need some sort of focus or concentration as an MBA, and you might be encouraged to choose your functional area early since MBA recruiting starts soon after you set foot on campus. Realize, however, that once you start working, you will be exposed to many interesting jobs and career paths that you had *no idea* existed while you were in business school. Besides, the boundaries between traditional functional areas are fragile. Explore how fluid these boundaries are and bridge them. The MBA degree itself is interdisciplinary and flexible, as is the current work environment. Many marketing employees are doing what seems to be finance work. They are crunching numbers and using Excel and statistical tools to help predict new-product sales. Many finance professionals spend more time acting as internal strategy consultants than utilizing pure finance skills. The buckets are blurring, and it's sometimes hard to know who is doing what. Your chosen functional area may have very little relevance five years into your career. Smart companies are looking for people who are well rounded and have the intelligence and adaptability to perform in different functions as the needs of an organization evolve.

Maximize Use of Your Own Career Center

What a luxury! Full-time MBA students often receive dedicated, exclusive support from career-center professionals. Students from other majors generally don't have access to the breadth and depth of career services that full-time MBAs enjoy. Some business school career centers even have dedicated professionals who provide extra support for international students. Leverage the great resources available to you and, of course, develop a strong relationship with your career advisor. If managed correctly, your relationship with your advisor can continue to grow and strengthen after you finish your MBA. When it's time to make a career change or switch jobs, your MBA career coach can serve as a great sounding board as well as a source of job leads.

Be Interesting

This is critical! Your career interests are yours, but they're probably not unique. MBAs come and go. Some dream about a hot investment job in New York with Goldman Sachs, a few dream of being a consultant with McKinsey or Bain, and many would kill for a career with Amazon or Google. A new MBA class brings new faces and names but familiar stories and dreams. Don't be just another MBA. You must have a great sense of who you are and where you best fit, but you'll need more than that to secure a great U.S. job. Share your interests, hobbies, fears, dreams, and insights with those you meet. Business is about relationships, connecting with people, and instilling trust. U.S recruiting and hiring managers must feel you have good people skills. You are fresh and international. If you want to stand out, tell your true story. International MBAs can be so career-focused that they often forget how to have a normal conversation. Revisit some of the ideas from Chapters 5 and 6 and put them into practice. Employers *want* to hire interesting people.

Always Think Impact

Impact is key. This is what should keep you up at night. *Where can you make a difference?* If you know the answer, you can greatly increase your chances of securing a job in the United States.

Inventory Your Skill Set

Identify existing skills. You will need to leverage as much of your pre-MBA strengths and knowledge as possible in order to be competitive and show companies that you're worth sponsoring. This should be your main priority. As a secondary goal, identify any gaps in your skill set and develop a plan to address them through club involvement, professional organizations, or focused electives. Pre-MBA experiences must be leveraged correctly for you to succeed. If you're not getting interviews, ask yourself: am I leveraging my proven strengths and skills as much as possible?

Divide Your Career Focus into Buckets

Someone interested in technology might seek jobs in consulting, technical project management, or even sales with technology manufacturers that seek professionals with strong customer-facing skills and technical expertise. The point is to open up additional doors to make success more likely.

Possibly Target Multiple Fields

An inventory of your pre-MBA skills may reveal that you can successfully compete for jobs in different industries and functional areas. Does the idea of targeting more than one field make you nervous? It probably does, because it seems you'll lose focus. Be careful when implementing this strategy to ensure you don't come across as undecided or even desperate. Widening your pool of options to increase interview opportunities is important since interview opportunities can be so limited for international students. An international student from India I knew, for example, targeted roles in consulting as well as marketing analytics. Both functional areas leveraged some of the same core strengths he had, and since he was competitive in both fields, he multiplied his interview offers. Expanding your job search can only help you, but often it requires more effort. Casting a wide net takes a considerable amount of energy, creativity, and planning, as well as the help of a career coach or mentor who has a good understanding of your value and the transferability of your skill set and work experiences.

Reach for Your Dreams, but Have a Backup Plan

In today's economy, international MBA job hunters need a plan A, B, and sometimes C if they plan on staying in the United States after graduation.

Market Your Skills

Successfully marketing your existing skills to recruiters and hiring managers will be critical for your success. As an international student, focus on swiftly explaining the source of your natural strengths, many of which are gifts provided by your culture and cannot easily be replicated by your competition. Embrace your cultural strengths and use them as a valid tool to get hired.

Network Like Crazy

The MBA degree presents a wonderful excuse for international students to network with U.S. business professionals and build a base of contacts. Prioritize networking so you can eventually get in front of the right people, tell them your story, and let them know what you're ready to accomplish. It may be incredibly hard to watch your grades suffer while you focus on your job search; but be sure to allocate appropriate time for networking. Have as many informational interviews as you can. I suggest at least one a week, preferably two. It's key that you develop contacts inside your target firms, particularly well-known global firms that international MBAs are normally motivated to target. Reach out often. Be persistent. Have thick skin. Prepare before reaching out. Utilize the frameworks laid out in this book so people will fall in love with you when you speak with them, and become vested in your success. Don't be too focused on perfecting your resume or writing the best cover letter possible at the expense of spending time with individuals who work at the firms you are targeting. This is usually the best way to secure an interview and get hired.

Assess Your Chances

Understand how friendly or unfriendly your field of interest may be for international students. Certain areas of supply chain require knowledge of import/export regulations and language skills, positioning international students well to succeed—as opposed to some areas of finance, for example, which is an industry that may require in-depth knowledge of certain regulatory requirements, such as GAAP, that many international students don't have expertise in. Similarly, certain roles in marketing, such as brand management, may be more on the creative side, may have a high supply of domestic candidates, and often require strong verbal and cultural fluency. Marketing analytics, on the other hand, is a more technical field where competency and ability to perform specific functions like data modeling may be more critical than delivering a flawless presentation in front of a group. Consulting and banking normally do sponsor because they're global, have international clients, and often need to move people around the world.

Leverage Your Language Skills

Target jobs that require languages you speak, particularly if you're from a BRIC country. I am often surprised by how underutilized this effective job-search strategy is. Many jobs may require command of Mandarin, for example, given the important role China plays in today's global economy. Seek roles in firms that do business with your country, which may allow you to use your language skills. Google "Mandarin marketing jobs" or utilize job boards such as Indeed.com or Linkedin and see what you find, for instance. Create contacts inside companies that have posted jobs with language requirements you can meet.

Leverage Your Quantitative Skills

MBAs with STEM skills are in demand, particularly when they are able to apply these skills in high-growth industries like healthcare and technology. Whenever possible, combine functional area expertise or interest with industry knowledge, as well as one or two in-demand hard skills. Sprinkle language skills on top when possible, and you will end up with a winning formula for securing a great H-1B job. If you like marketing, for example, knowing how to perform an SQL query and having a knack for Excel and in-demand statistical packages can be powerful. It's even better if you can utilize your language skills to help a firm sell more products or services in your home region. International MBAs with aptitude for data crunching will have quality jobs to target, some of which may clearly state that they welcome international students as applicants. Take a look at this example from Capitol One, which I found listed on Indeed by typing in the keywords "data, MBA, quantitative":

Sr. Operations Analyst (USA)

Primary Location: Plano, TX

Job Description: Does the idea of analyzing complex data inspire you? Are you ready to make smart decisions that result in superior business solutions? As a Senior Operations Analyst at Capitol One, you can achieve things you never thought possible. [...]

Preferred Qualifications:

• Masters Degree or MBA

• Lean or Six Sigma process engineering certification

• 3+ years experience in analysis (qualitative and quantitative)

- 2+ years experience in working with databases and manipulating data

- 2+ years experience in meeting facilitation and presentation delivery

- 2+ years experience in MS Office (focus on advanced Excel)

Capitol One will consider sponsoring a new qualified applicant for employment authorization for this position.

You may find a marketing job (e.g., business intelligence analyst, quantitative analyst, or pricing and revenue optimization analyst) that allows you to play with numbers in a challenging way and utilize your newly acquired MBA skills. Marketing today is all about analytics. Consultants make recommendations based on numbers, not their gut feeling. Analytics cuts across several different industries: banking, consulting, higher education, and government, among others. Amazon is not the only company that relies on analytics to recommend new products and services for consumers. Just about every MBA job out there seems to include "analytical skills" as a preferred or required qualification. These skills are in demand and they are in short supply. Accounting has long been known as the language of business, and analytics has emerged as a similar phenomenon, where science and art intersect. This type of rigor in decision making could be great news for quant-savvy international MBAs. The "art" aspect of analytics can also be a good fit for many international students, whose biculturalism and strong cognitive abilities enable them to discern patterns and themes that may go unnoticed by others.

Communication skills will always matter—they're the #1 skill employers look for in MBAs according to GMAC's 2014 Corporate Recruiters Survey Report[1]—but you may impress a recruiter or hiring manager by

---

[1] Reproduced with the permission of the Graduate Management Admission Council® (GMAC). The 2014 *Corporate Recruiters Survey Report* is available at: www.gmac.com/corporaterecruites

displaying a knack for data manipulation or an ability to merge databases and extract value from them. Recruiters may not easily find these abilities in other candidates. You don't have to be a statistician to handle these jobs. Many international MBAs can use their quantitative and technical background to "translate" an algorithm that predicts the future use of electricity in U.S. households, for example. When the results of an analysis look questionable, you can assess the variables utilized in the model, the statistical approach, and the tools that were used to conduct the analysis, and issue an intelligent opinion about the model and maybe make recommendations for improvement. You'll impress employers with your confidence in making strategic recommendations and driving the kind of change that is often expected of MBAs.

Look for firms and industries that place a great deal of value on analyzing huge amounts of data to drive smart business decisions. The credit card industry and the airline business are obvious choices. Visa and American Airlines, for example, have a strong track record of pursing H-1B visas for roles that could require an MBA. Industries like healthcare and transportation (e.g., FedEx) are also interesting choices.

Of course, international MBAs also have a great chance of securing quality H-1B jobs in quasi-technical positions that tap into their technical background. A little bit of programming or data management experience will never hurt.

Career Changers

Many international MBAs are looking to switch careers. Sometimes it can be challenging to change industry and functional areas at the same time without a strong base of contacts in the United States, while simultaneously learning how to live life in a new country. If you were a teacher in your home country and are now getting an MBA with an eye toward marketing roles, targeting marketing jobs in the education sector may be more productive than trying to break into CPG, where you lack both industry and functional area experience. When possible, as a career transitioner, use your language skills as a way to differentiate and draw more attention to yourself as a candidate. Find roles that take advantage of that.

Stepping-Stone Approach

Assess with your career coach and mentors the likelihood of attaining your job-search goals. Your first job post-MBA may be a stepping stone toward a position that more closely aligns with your passion, interests, and skills, particularly if you're a career changer. Many international MBAs report that a career change is a lot harder than they anticipated. An MBA and willpower aren't enough; many recruiters are looking for experience. If you want to go into finance and you have no experience in the field, you may have problems, as an example. If it takes you a little longer to achieve your career goals, don't despair. As long as you're moving in the right direction and strengthening your skill set along the way, you're doing well.

As we discussed in Chapter 12, "The Big, Bad Visa Chapter," transferring to another company as an H-1B worker is often not as hard as securing your first H-1B job. Many firms that have a "we don't sponsor" policy are happy to accept H-1B transfers. As an MBA, leverage the H-1B portability rules. Your first MBA job may not last as long as you think.

Job Titles: A Word of Warning

Don't be too fixated on chasing specific job titles. Stop identifying your-self with one. You are not a business analyst. You are not a marketing manager. You are an individual with passions and interests, and you have skills and work experiences that may apply to multiple job titles. This is a key mentality for international students, because you need to increase your pool of interview opportunities. Be focused, but don't limit your opportunities by telling people that you want to be a product manager.

U.S. job titles often don't mean what you think they do. A recent MBA graduate I know got a job with HP, and his job title is Sales Engineer Operational Analyst. This individual is not an engineer, and he told me he never intended to become one. Many interesting roles, some of which you may not know about, can make full use of your interests and MBA skills. A role as a channel marketing manager can be exciting and make full use of your MBA skills, but this job title is often unknown to international MBAs. If you focus on your skill set and impact, your coach can help you identify potential jobs to target that you may not know about, broadening your pool of opportunities.

MBA Career Fairs

Here are a few recommendations regarding MBA career fairs like Black MBA and National Society of Hispanic MBAs (NSHMBA):

- Plan on attending at least one of these major MBA career fairs.

- There will certainly be many firms at these events that don't sponsor, but some will. Research which firms may be open to sponsoring ahead of time and be ready to talk to them at the fair if you are interested in what they do and feel you can help them. Prepare thoroughly, and use **www.myvisajobs.com** to get a feel for the sponsorship track record of the firms you are targeting.

- Apply to positions early. This is critical, as it helps you secure interviews in advance of attending one of these job fairs.

- Make mistakes. Learn how to speak with recruiters. Learn how hard it is to tell people what you want to do with your life in 30 seconds. Listen to yourself as you speak. Do you believe what you're saying?

- When targeting well-know firms at job fairs such as Microsoft and Amazon, if mobile, make it clear to whom you are talking to that you are willing to explore job opportunities outside of the U.S.

- Meet international students from different schools. Don't spend your entire time hanging out with your peers. Create new relationships. Make an effort to remain in touch with people after the fair.

- Introduce yourself to career coaches from different schools and ask them what they're doing to help their international students. Share what your school is doing to help people like you. Have interesting conversations and make new connections. Learn.

Going Home

The material covered in Chapter 14, "The Chapter You Don't Want to Read: Returning Home After Graduation," fully applies to MBAs. If there is little market demand for your skills and profile, or high competition for the types of jobs you're interested in, you may want to manage two job searches simultaneously: one for a great job at home, and one for a role in the United States. If your first job post-MBA ends up being at home, that may work out more than well in the end. Several global talent surveys indicate that there is a severe talent gap in countries like China and Brazil, particularly among the ranks of senior management. You can make big bucks in emerging countries these days as an MBA with American managerial skills, particularly if you move into some sort of managerial role.

Ten Common Job-Hunting Challenges and How to Overcome Them

While this is not an exhaustive list, these are the traits and behaviors I've observed over the years that have prevented many international MBA students from having a fair chance of securing a great H-1B job after graduation:

1) Poor language skills

Strong language skills are *essential* for MBAs. Precise communication is highly valued in the U.S. business context. In addition to managing how your accent, intonation, speed, and volume of speech impact how you're perceived and how effective you might be as a business leader, you must also consider how your natural communication style matches Americans' expectations. Some people are direct communicators (preferred in the United States), while others communicate in a more subtle way. Some MBA jobs require higher levels of communication skills than others. Students interested in consulting should develop assertive communication skills and learn how to articulate their thoughts convincingly. Strong communication skills are a critical factor in whether you'll advance your career in the United States. They're also closely tied to soft skills, which are highly valued by MBA recruiters. Ask for feedback regarding your communication skills, and take the necessary steps to improve, such as enrolling in an advanced business communication class while analyzing how your natural communication style compares to how Americans normally communicate.

2) Lack of U.S. work experience

In certain cases, your student visa might allow you to work off-campus as a second-year MBA. (Always check with your university before accepting any type of employment as an international student, even if it's unpaid, such as a volunteer opportunity.) When possible, try working a few hours a week or take on a short-term consulting assignment that gives you U.S. work experience. When you interview for full-time positions as a second-year MBA, you'll attract the attention of recruiters and hiring managers if you can demonstrate that you've gained U.S. work experience during your studies.

3) Sloppy cover letter, resume, and emails

Nobody expects a non-English speaker to write perfectly 100% of the time. Americans themselves don't do it, and you and I probably don't, either, in our native language. However, error-free messages with the right tone are critical when you're in the middle of a recruitment process. There's no compromising there. Be professional. Stick with simple sentences; don't try to get too creative with your writing. When in doubt, ask a friendly U.S. colleague to review what you wrote before you press the send button.

4) Failure to network

Since you read Chapter 5, "Networking," you know how to build rapport and trust when engaging with others. And when you secure that initial informational interview, you know how to handle it. You want to come across as very prepared and extremely professional, and with a high desire to learn.

5) Using a canned approach when connecting with people

"I'm interested in becoming a product manager" is a typical phrase used by many international MBAs. Introduce yourself differently when meeting others and be much more personable. People are attracted to and comfortable with those who are spontaneous. This is key to your success as an MBA. As you know, your international knowledge and awareness are critical traits. Don't be robotic or rehearsed, and try not to say something that one hundred other MBAs have said before. Be yourself. Your story is unique and interesting, so share it.

6) Conventional interview preparation

Remember to be creative and at times, when possible, mix and match interview strategies that suit you so you can successfully deliver what interviewers are looking for. Reflect back on Fang Wang's success.

7) Restricted job search in terms of company targets, position focus, and geography

If the labor market in your chosen area is flooded (the demand for employees is far less than the number of job seekers), it is particularly important to think outside the box and explore alternative options.

8) Too much reliance on campus recruiting

While it is possible that your dream company will come to your university to interview you, it is normally best to proactively try to connect with the right individuals who can help you achieve your job search goals. Now that you have read *The International Advantage*, you know how to make this kind of outreach.

9) Inadequate search time

Different students will need to dedicate different amounts of time and energy to their job search. Students looking for a job that's similar to what they had for several years before their MBA studies might be able to focus more on identifying targets. Career transitioners will need to devote more job-search time and build experience and general know-how. Regardless of your situation, looking for a job requires an active approach, not a passive one. Unless you're a superstar with highly in-demand skills, you won't just be given the job you deserve; you'll have to go after it.

10) Too few references

While not a deal breaker, create a pool of U.S. references. Professors, alumni, and university staff may be the most obvious potential references. Getting references from around the world on social-media profiles is helpful, though, especially if the referral comes from someone with multinational experience in well-known companies in the industry and functional area you're targeting.

Sometimes your U.S. references can brag for you better than you are able to brag about yourself. Your references can't be with you at your job interview, but they might be able to open an initial door, which is sometimes the hardest step for international students: cracking the door open. If you feel you've developed good rapport with someone you worked closely with who got to know your strengths, weaknesses, and work style, it's okay to ask them if they'll serve as a reference for you. I've been a reference for many MBAs I've coached in the past.

16

7 Common Job-Search Mistakes New International MBAs Make

Coming to the U.S. to pursue an MBA as an international student is a huge accomplishment. You should feel very proud that you are where you are. However, don't forget that you have a lot of work ahead of you, especially if you'll be seeking U.S. employment after graduation. To that end, here are some common job-search mistakes to avoid as you march toward your career goals.

Mistake #1: Feeling overconfident

The start of the MBA degree is a festive and beautiful moment in the life of an international student. Without the stress of classes, you're able to celebrate getting into b-school and connect with your new colleagues while dreaming about high-paying jobs with big-name firms. It's easy to feel that everything will go smoothly and that your efforts and talents will be enough to overcome any job search challenges that might lie ahead.

Solution: Don't rest on your laurels. Don't assume for a second that all the hard work is done and now all you have to do is get good grades and wait for firms to come to your campus, interview you, and offer you a job. Getting accepted into a top MBA program and securing a high-paying H-1B job are two very different things. Instead of feeling invincible, take a conservative posture early on in your MBA studies and ask yourself, "What could derail of me? Am I possibly already off track and not aware of it? How can I avoid the dreadful scenario of having an MBA diploma on my hands but no job offers? What can I do early on in my studies to set up myself up for a great H-1B job come graduation?" Start getting answers to these questions by fully leveraging your career center resources.

Mistake #2: Positioning yourself as a generalist

Most schools describe the MBA degree as a general degree. You learn a little bit of finance, marketing, general management, and maybe supply chain. And therein lies the great danger for international MBA students who want to work in the U.S. after graduation. As an international MBA seeking U.S. employment, you don't want to be perceived as a generalist by recruiters and hiring managers. A generic MBA profile that can easily be found anywhere could be the kiss of death for international MBAs seeking H-1B employment.

Solution: Be a specialist, not a generalist. Find your sustainable competitive advantages early on in the MBA program and build on these capabilities going forward. Focus on clarifying your interests, skills, experiences, and languages skills early in the program. Realize that interplay between these can be complex. And double down on your international advantages. Find your niche and own it. Analyze your profile through the lenses of employers and always signal differentiation, specialization, and depth to the market.

Mistake #3: Overvaluing your MBA

You might have heard this before: an MBA on its own is not enough of a differentiator, even if you're getting your degree from Harvard or Stanford. The MBA is certainly not a guaranteed of employment. The degree may have been popular in the 1980s, but it's under much pressure these days, as hiring managers and recruiters realize that there are several different ways to acquire knowledge and skills these days. In fact, it's not just the MBA degree that's under pressure, it's the entire formal higher educational system in the U.S.

This past March, Apple CEO Tim Cook attended an American Workforce Policy Advisory Board meeting in Washington, D.C., and while sitting next to President Donald Trump, Cook said that about 50 percent of Apple's hires lacked a formal four-year college degree.

Solution: As a recently arrived international MBA, start to construct a narrative that highlights how the power of an MBA education complements what you've done prior to coming to the U.S. If you can do this, U.S. employers will take notice and your MBA will play an important role in helping you get hired.

Mistake #4: Overvaluing your degree specialization

I've interviewed many MBAs who proudly told me that that they obtained an MBA with a specialization in finance, for example. Even in the areas where MBAs say they've "specialized," sometimes I've found their level of knowledge and skill to be little more than rudimentary or not significantly differentiated from an undergrads' knowledge. In addition, MBAs sometimes forget that they might also be competing with other master's degree candidates with graduate degrees in statistics, mathematics, and economics.

Solution: An MBA specialization might help, but it might not be enough. Supplement your skill set and demonstrate more muscle power in areas you're interested in. Go beyond the traditional MBA curriculum and gain deeper knowledge and confidence in important areas that could separate you from the crowd. Free courses on Udemy and Coursera can help fill the gaps in your profile and help enhance your competiveness. Savvy international MBAs leverage their strong cognitive abilities to quickly pick up hard skills on their own that might differentiate them from other competitors. You don't need to take a full college course to learn Tableau; for example. A few hours of investment may be all you need to get you started. Watch a few YouTube videos and get going.

Mistake #5: Not taking hard skills seriously

You might naively believe that, as an MBA, your job is to let others worry about data crunching and the more technical aspects related to a project, and that your role is to focus on strategy—acting as the interface between the technical and product teams, talking to clients, and delivering powerful, crisp presentations. Remember that, in general, tech companies are reluctant to hire managers who lack hard skills, so MBA grads who spent some time working as a programmer or engineer before attending business school are more attractive candidates for management positions at tech firms than MBA degree recipients without that experience.

Solution: Treat any MBA job, regardless of functional area or industry, as a technology job. Even outside of tech, hard skills matter. Skills in coding and analytics can get you noticed as a candidate. Technical skills have the added bonus of improving your general problem-solving and decision-making skills because they provide more rigor to your thinking. Knowledge of analytics is also beneficial. Start by picking up advanced MS-Excel skills and move on from there. Add some VBA to the picture perhaps. You don't have to be super great at the technical stuff. Know enough to handle most ordinary situations. Knowing enough already puts you ahead of the pack and will make it look a magician in front of hiring managers and your peers.

Mistake #6: Thinking too much like an MBA

MBAs can look alike, think alike, and talk alike. They're taught how to interview the same way and they basically take the same classes and use the same textbooks. This can result in MBAs sounding rehearsed and robotized, like people who've memorized a framework from classes they took and are eager to showcase their new knowledge during job interviews.

Solution: Impress U.S. hiring managers with bold, fresh, non-MBA thinking that can help their businesses explode. Differentiation is the name of the game, and you have to think outside the box and connect the dots better than other candidates. Careful with traditional MBA speak. Showcase your global thinking and superior cognitive abilities. Leverage the full force of your multicultural brain. Let your international advantages guide you. After speaking with U.S. hiring managers, leave them with a feeling of "Wow, this is not your typical MBA."

Mistake #7: Placing too much focus on job title

Let me guess: perhaps you're interested in becoming a product manager or know international MBAs who will be targeting jobs with this job title? And you or they plan to accept nothing less than a product manager role upon graduation? Be careful not to limit yourself!

Solution: Instead of targeting jobs with specific jobs titles you might like now, savvy international MBAs focus on identifying quality firms they might want to join. First, get your foot in the door with a great company that sponsors and might want to give you an H-1B visa, no matter what job they may be interested in giving you. Worry more about finding the right job fit and worry much less about what your job title will be. Joining a good firm is much more important than focusing on getting a job with the job title you've always dreamed of.

For example, if you're interested in technology, would you turn down Microsoft if they asked you to join their cloud-computing group as a sales professional because you're good with clients, already understand the power of cloud computing, and know how to translate the benefits of this emerging technology to business value for firms?

There's great mobility in corporate America. With results, patience, and some corporate savvy, you can easily migrate to the group and job of your dreams *once you join the right organization* and secure your H-1B visa. The product manager job title can wait, but don't be surprised if your desire to pursue a job you're in love with now vanishes once you get your first job in the U.S. after b-school. Once you enter corporate America you'll discover a ton of roles that look interesting and excite you and that you never knew existed while pursuing your MBA.

17

Choosing The Right Company Targets

Newly arrived international MBA students usually rush to find a list of firms that have sponsored in the past, or firms that have come to campus to recruit and that were open to interviewing international students. While it makes sense to leverage your career center's resources to quickly learn these names, don't limit yourself to these firms. With time on your side, you have the luxury of forgetting about sponsorship for a while.

Focus on creating a target list of firms based on your interests and your belief that you can positively impact their operations, *regardless of whether they sponsor*. Initially, as a first-year MBA, you're not necessarily building your list in order to get hired, although that could happen. You're building a list of firms to help you get smart about the types of jobs you think you may want to pursue, to learn more about a particular industry, and to start developing U.S. contacts.

You're new to the United States, and the world of U.S. work is mostly unknown to you. Operate with an open mind.

You're 100% in learning mode. It's about proactively making contacts inside interesting firms *before* applying for jobs, *before* a job opening is even advertised.

How many organizations should you have on your target list? The number of companies you may want to target will depend on factors such as whether or not you are a career transitioner, the type of roles you are seeking, the kind of profile you have, the brand of your school, your knowledge of the industry and sector you want to break into, and even your ability to effectively manage your target list. I have worked with successful international MBA students who had as few as 10 firms on their target list throughout their studies. Others I felt needed to manage a much larger list of target companies.

In the spirit of providing generic advice that must be validated by your career coach so it can be customized for you, I recommend you maintain an ongoing list of about 15 to 20 organizations that you are actively researching and seeking professional connections within. Track the firms on an Excel spreadsheet to stay organized. Maintain a log of when you contacted people at these firms and the overall outcome of the conversations.

Build Your Initial Target List

What companies do you target? Let's use a practical example to illustrate a very simple methodology you can use to determine what firms or jobs you want to target. Let's say you love e-commerce. You've always been interested in this field, and you already have some strong digital marketing skills, so you go ahead and add Amazon to your target list. It also makes sense to add organizations with similar business models to Amazon's, such as Ebay, Alibaba, Groupon, and Overstock. Think economies of scale whenever possible when generating an initial target list. Start with what you like to do.

Next, define existing skills you have that you want to use in the roles you seek.

Is there a particular industry you like and maybe have experience with? Education? Energy? Fashion? Technology? Many international MBA students have found great success creating target lists around a particular industry that they already have knowledge about or passion for.

Indeed and other job-search boards can be great tools to leverage when creating your initial target list. Use them to identify roles you're interested in by searching for jobs that preferably leverage skills you already have. When you get an interesting hit, study the company and see if you want to add it to your target list. I once worked with an MBA student from Thailand who came into the program with strong CAD drawing skills, which he wanted to continue using in his post-MBA job. He created a great target list of firms that had quality MBA job openings listing CAD as a required skill.

Sometimes all you need is the name of one large company to get started. Google will automatically highlight similar companies when you search for the name of your initial target. Look for the "People also search for" feature. Give it a try and see if you can uncover interesting company targets that you didn't know existed.

Research the Targets

After generating an initial set of targets, research the firms to get a sense of what they do. Go deep into the research. Understand how the firms innovate, build relationships with other firms, and market their products and services. Look for answers to some basic questions:

- What is the firm's position in the marketplace?

- How do you feel about their products and services compared to their competitors'?

- Are they expanding or already doing business internationally? Do they have a presence in your home country? It might be interesting if they do.

- Do they need to partner with other firms in order to complete their offerings? Many large firms do. For example, it is widely known that Amazon lets third-party sellers leverage the capabilities of their e-commerce engine. Large firms that many MBAs are interested in, such as Ebay, Amazon, and Google, have created a rich ecosystem of co-dependent firms. Similarly, technology manufacturers like Cisco, IBM, and HP often open their platforms and develop interoperability testing with other players in the marketplace. Who are these firms? Find out the names. No matter what industry or type of firm you're targeting, they likely don't exist in a vacuum. They often need to partner or go to market with other firms to complete their offerings and provide their clients with superior value. These lesser-known companies may be interesting targets, so add them to your list. Get to know your field or sector of interest beyond the names that appear on the news.

- When you click the "careers" link on the websites of your target firms, what kinds of jobs do they seem to be hiring for? Could they use someone with your background on their team?

- When you review the LinkedIn profiles of the people who work at the firms you want to target, can you relate to their career trajectories?

After you find answers to these initial questions, if you still feel excited about the firms you picked, and feel you could be a match for them, keep them on your list. If not, drop the names that don't seem worth investigating further and replace them.

Make Connections Inside Your Target Firms

Once you've created your initial list of firms and completed an appropriate amount of research, your second task is to connect with people who have inspiring career paths inside the firms you picked. This can be a difficult part of the job-search process for international students. Several techniques were outlined in this book that can help you with this outreach effort. Remember: you have something interesting to share with others. You are different, and you are fresh. Alumni contacts inside the target firms may be helpful, but they're certainly not required. What is most critical is that you contact people in a genuine way. Chapter 5, "Networking," outlines several frameworks you can use when contacting people. Because you're starting early, you have enough time to keep in touch with the people you contact and nurture your relationship with them during your MBA studies. This could be a great step toward building a strong base of contacts in the United States.

For large well-known multinationals where the competition for MBA jobs is always intense, identifying individuals inside these organizations that have jobs with links to your home country is smart. You already know that you have a clear competitive advantage for certain roles due to local expertise, work authorization, cultural savvy, and language fluency. Network with professionals who know what's going on in your home region. Use LinkedIn to identify these professionals and reach out to them when you're ready.

Target List As Risk Management

Diversification is the name of the game for many students. In general, keep the following in mind: you didn't apply for only one MBA program when you were thinking of coming to the United States. You may have had a list of preferred schools that you thought was going to be tough to get into, and you probably managed a list of schools you thought your odds of getting in were pretty good. You may not have applied to Harvard or Stanford because you were pretty certain you wouldn't get in. Apply the same mindset when choosing what companies to target. Develop a target list based on reason instead of emotion. Smart investment strategies diversify assets across a range of assets to minimize risk. This is exactly the position you may want to take when developing a strong target list that minimizes the risk of you having to go home after graduation. The idea is to leave no stone unturned and explore every option with an open mind.

What follows is a simple methodology you can use to create a good target list.

Target #1: Start-Ups or Small Firms (1 – 2 Names)

Start-ups are certainly not a fit for everybody, and they may have inherent risk factors that can be particularly tricky for international students. Few international MBAs seem interested in start-up firms. But as an international student willing to explore all options, don't discard start-ups too quickly. If you fit with the company culture and employees and believe you can help the company grow, who knows? If you find a small firm that has plans to export a product or service to your country, they might be able to create an exciting MBA-grade role for you. Your university may have connections with local start-ups that need MBA talent to help them grow. In the spirit of keeping all options open, add one or two start-ups to your target list.

The level of innovation among young entrepreneurs in the United States is amazing. Ask these talented, fearless individuals if they wish to work for a large, well-established firm and watch their reactions. These folks move fast and want to be part of something big. Maybe you find excitement in this space as well. Once again, the start-up environment is not for everybody. Do your due diligence as if you were an investor, and discuss with your career advisor whether an unknown company on your resume could become a barrier to future career development.

Target #2: Mid-Size Companies (5 – 6 Names)

This can be the secret layer, a very important group of companies to target, but one that normally does not receive the level of attention it deserves. Even though international MBAs tend to be more comfortable with mid-size firms than start-ups, the level of focus on these firms is usually inadequate. Remember to research private mid-size organizations that are reputable, have steady management teams, and offer quality jobs.

Pick a few mid-size firms that you're passionate about *early* on in your job search—not the month before you graduate, after everything else has failed—and work diligently to create connections inside these firms. Don't treat them as backups. They are viable options, and you should pursue them aggressively.

Small or mid-size organizations have few layers of hierarchy and a simplified decision-making process. Even if you're unsure whether a smaller firm you like is open to sponsoring, pursue it if you feel it's a fit for you. If a smaller firm likes you, it will sometimes move forward quickly and hire you. Compare this mentality with the culture that can exist in large corporations that don't hire international students. Large firms have detailed hiring policies built into their system, making it difficult for them to change their hiring policy to hire someone who needs an H-1B visa. While not impossible, it may be very hard to be granted an exception.

In general, move on if a large firm you're interested in does not sponsor. It's usually not worth your time, unless you have strong advocacy from a hiring manager who needs your skill set.

Many small and mid-size firms may not know that they can hire international students. One mid-size company owner I talked to during a job fair told me: "I thought only Bill Gates and Google could hire international students. I didn't know this option was open to me." These firms may have no clue what it takes to get work authorization for an employee, but don't let this obstacle dissuade you from pursuing them.

Find the Names

To uncover names of quality mid-size firms, peruse the database at www. inc.com/inc5000/index.html. Forbes also publishes a list every year at www.forbes.com/best-small-companies/list/. A quick Google search may reveal a list of companies in a sector you're interested in that someone has already compiled. Leverage online information to uncover off-the-beaten-path company names you may want to learn more about, and add them to your target list. When meeting people who know your career goals and interests, ask them, "Have you heard of any interesting firms I should target?"

Job opportunities with smaller firms are not designed for university recruiting, and these firms may not call your school to advertise a good MBA job. You have to go after these firms yourself. Several students report that these firms are usually more open to a "cold call" for an informational interview because they receive less pressure from MBAs.

The Power of Mid-Size Firms

If you get to know the sector and broader market you're interested in, you will come to appreciate just how threatening mid-size firms can be to larger firms that they compete against and that MBAs normally prefer to target. Ask someone who works at Salesforce if they take Sugar CRM seriously as a competitor. These firms offer lower price points and focus on smaller customers who can't afford enterprise-class offerings provided by big-name companies, and they often need talented MBAs help them grow. They often "poach" seasoned professionals from established players.

Havish's Story

By luck, everything worked out for Havish, an international MBA student from India I worked closely with for two years. Havish was one of the very last students from his class to get a job. He was determined to work for a large company, preferably as a consultant or a product manager, and strongly resisted my advice to target mid-size firms and expand his targets beyond the biggest names. I asked Havish to speak with a few people who, like him, had initially targeted large firms but had found fulfilling, lucrative careers with smaller firms that most of us have never heard of. Havish thanked me for the opportunity to have these conversations but politely reminded me that large names were still his focus. I have many stories about international MBA students who rolled the dice until the last minute, but none have the drama of Havish's tale.

Right after graduation, confronted with the reality that he still didn't have a job, he panicked. "I don't want to go home," he told me. He agreed to explore all options and inform his classmates and contacts that he was very open to exploring challenging roles with smaller firms. A week after Havish sent an email to his peers asking for assistance, a classmate informed him of an interesting marketing role posted on LinkedIn. He decided to apply for the position, though, in my opinion, he wasn't very enthusiastic at first. He managed to contact the recruiter via LinkedIn and did receive a call for an interview. He had never heard of the organization before, so I don't think he took them too seriously initially. However, as the interview process progressed and Havish learned more about the firm, he became very excited about it. In the end, he was offered the job, accepted the position, and loves what he does now. Havish is off to a great start in his marketing career. He is now working for a stable mid-size firm with about 300 employees and a reputation for being one of the best mid-size firms to work for in the United States. Initially, he had no idea he was about to join an awesome firm. Today he's a happy and productive H-1B worker.

Take Off Your Blinders

If you want to stay in the United States but feel uncomfortable with the prospect of accepting a job with a company that you, your family, or your classmates have never heard of, you may want to take your blinders off and be more flexible so you don't unnecessarily run the risk of going home after graduation. Many international students keep striving for the top-tier names—that is, until graduation approaches and time has almost run out.

According to a report published in July 2012 called "The Search for Skills: Demand for H-1B Immigrant Workers in U.S. Metropolitan Areas" by the D.C.-based Brookings Institution, "the 100 highest requesting employers of H-1B visas in 2010 – 2011 account for 20% of national demand." A small number of employers are heavy users of the H-1B program. We can use the 80/20 rule economists created to evaluate the distribution of H-1B visa filings. The higher requesting employers of H-1B visas are firms that international MBAs often wish to work for. They include familiar names like Microsoft, Intel, and Google; financial services firms like JPMorgan and Goldman Sachs; and consulting firms like Deloitte.

According to the same report, almost half of the employers who filed an H-1B petition in 2010 and 2011 requested only one worker, and 94% requested fewer than 10. These are very interesting statistics, clearly showing that firms most of us have never heard of are users of the H-1B program. These are firms international students should learn about. Many are surprised to hear that most H-1B filings may come from unknown firms. These firms seem to be hiring H-1B workers—selectively and in small quantities, but they are hiring. Consider adding these firms to your target list if you feel you're a match for them. Check www.myvisajobs. com for a list of companies that have sponsored in the past. Remember that big-name firms that hire a lot of H-1B workers account for only 20% of the national demand.

Target #3: Companies Known to Hire Internationals (7 – 10 Names)

MBAs in general, and international MBAs in particular, are drawn to big-name global firms. With a global reach and progressive hiring practices, these firms tend to hire the best people they can find and welcome MBA candidates who need a work visa.

U.S. Firms With a Global Footprint

U.S. firms that have offices in places like Singapore, Canada, Australia, or Hong Kong, and that might be unwilling to sponsor you for an H-1B job in the United States, might be able to use your MBA talents in one of their English-speaking offices. Focus on your global mobility, and consider adding the names of quality U.S. firms that have a strong global footprint to your target list. Use the same concept when looking at top global names that may offer great career opportunities outside of the United States. Deloitte or Goldman Sachs may have skills gaps in certain parts of the world that you might be able to fill.

Additional Targets to Consider

Here are a few more possible areas to explore for company targets:

Companies Doing Business with Your Country

No matter where you're from, you should know the largest U.S. employers doing business with your country, as well as industries that are growing in your country that may need MBAs. My students from South Korea have kept me abreast of the exceptional technology oriented innovation their country is known for. Taiwanese students know that the semiconductor industry is hot. Chinese MBAs with an understanding of supply chain and cost-cutting manufacturing processes may be well positioned to target jobs that leverage their specific background and country competencies. Whatever your career interests are, whenever possible, tap into the rich body of knowledge your country may be known for and leverage it fully when job searching in the U.S. Share with those you meet best practices and innovation they may never have heard of. Educate those you talk to. U.S. firms that have a division/branch office in your home country can be interesting targets as well. Similarly, consider multinational firms from your country/region that might have operations in the United States.

Go Local

Remember to research companies close to where you're going to school. Companies are more likely to hire and interview candidates who are local.

Utilize Your Country's Embassy

Embassy employees are usually well connected and might be able to serve as great sources of leads and tips regarding what companies and industries to target. Reach out and ask for an informational interview. Embassies have dedicated personnel focused on "commercial activities" who might be able to provide you with valuable assistance when identifying firms to research. I once received a LinkedIn invite from an employee from the Embassy of Peru, whose job title is international business development. According to his profile, his office "promotes trade by identifying new opportunities for Peruvian exporters, facilitating contacts among key entrepreneurs, building more fruitful relations between Peruvian and American business organizations." What a great resource!

Beyond the Big Cities

Excited about living in South Dakota? Maybe you should be. Be willing to relocate to rural or underserved parts of the United States where companies may have a hard time hiring qualified professionals. It's almost always about supply and demand. While some of your American friends may have the luxury of dismissing the idea of working in the middle of nowhere, you should embrace this opportunity. The competition for jobs in popular cities is intense. Everyone wants to be in sunny California. Be open to all locations. You can search for top sponsors per state on www.myvisajobs.com.

Some pockets of the United States are seeing an influx of quality companies due to special tax incentives, and they need to attract high-caliber talent to fuel their growth. Certain states might be experiencing swift growth in key sectors. Things change fast, of course. Identify states that are becoming the "hot spots" or "clusters," attracting employers in your target industry or functional area that need to grow and may be having a tough time attracting quality workers. Silicon Valley is not the only hot area in the United States.

Neil Ruiz, Associate Fellow at The Brookings Institution, authored a report in August 2014 called "The Geography of Foreign Students in U .S Higher Education: Origins and Destinations, which I footnoted in Chapter 3. Neil, who has extensive research experience in topics related to international migration and U.S. immigration, believes that STEM international graduates in particular should explore opportunities in advanced manufacturing in the middle of America. "This is an interesting part of the U.S to target," says Neil. "Entrepreneurial-minded students should target RTP, located in North Carolina and also Colorado, Massachusetts, and of course Silicon Valley in California. These are examples of places that have employers who need to hire professionals with the type of skills international students normally have."

As a side note, use www.myvisajobs.com to access a list of past employers who have sponsored in the states listed above and consider adding them to your target list.

I asked Neil to share some specific job search advice with international students based on his research experience analyzing the distribution of H-1B visas, and this is what he had to say:

*"Technology is moving fast and companies are hiring H-1B work-
ers that are tech savvy, adjustable, and geographically mobile. This
combination of traits is not easy to find and international students
often have these characteristics. I think the key to success is to embrace the entrepreneurial spirit that the U.S is known for, and come
across as a candidate who's open to new ideas and possibilities, and
can function well in a very team-based work culture".*

Review and Rebalance

Your target list isn't set in stone. It's an evolving work, and you should
frequently step back to review and rebalance as needed. Of course, don't
be unnecessarily hasty in crossing names off: just because one email
brought no response doesn't mean hope is lost. Remember: have 15
names of firms you're actively working to learn more about and develop
connections with. Here are a few things to keep in mind whenever you
look over those names:

Get Practical

As graduation approaches, most large firms have completed their recruiting cycles; even if you're hoping for a just-in-time opportunity to open up
with a big-name global firm, shift your focus to firms that have a shorter
hiring cycle, have an advertised opening you fit, and might be open to
hiring international students. You may have started with Google on your
target list, but since a ton of Google hiring comes from internal referrals, if graduation is approaching and you still don't have a strong contact
inside the firm, it's time to drop the name.

As a second-year MBA, get practical and identify jobs and companies
that fit you and are open to hiring international students. Check www.

myvisajobs.com to see what companies have recently filed for H-1B visas and may have an interest in your profile and skill set. The contacts you made during your first year as an MBA can help you identify job openings and refer you to jobs. That's the ideal situation to be in. Don't be shy about leveraging your base of contacts even if you have not done a great job keeping in touch with them. Search for relevant companies in your field of interest and check their H-1B filing history and the type of positions for which they filed for H-1Bs. If you find a company whose sponsoring history focuses solely on technical jobs, don't necessarily rule them out if you have proven skills and differentiated knowledge that the firm may benefit from. Network with someone from the firm who understands your talents.

Leverage Extra Help

If you lack a strong base of contacts who can refer you to jobs, advertised openings will largely drive your job-search efforts as a second-year MBA. If you see a job that fits you, utilize your career-center resources wisely so they can try to connect with someone at the firm to draw attention to your application. Sometimes that's all international students need to be successful: a little bit of extra help cracking the door open.

The "ISEL" Formula Might Help You

With many of the international MBAs I have coached in the past, I have utilized the "ISEL" model to help them get focused on which jobs to target:

I = Interest (key for U.S. employers)

S = Skills (not always hard to develop if don't have them)

E = Experience (important for international job seekers)

L = Language (sometimes the winning weapon)

I $\Rightarrow$ S $\Rightarrow$ E $\Rightarrow$ L

Keep Impact Front and Center

Don't make the mistake of applying to companies *only* because they've sponsored in the past. While it can be reassuring and comforting to know that a company has a clear record of sponsoring MBAs, what good does that do if you lack the skills or work experience needed to land an interview? Approach companies because you can impact their business better than most people out there. Revisit the ISEL model as needed. If you offer true and differentiated value, then go for it and try to get hired. Think impact. Believe in yourself and the value you can bring to a firm.

Make Space for New Opportunities

Nothing ever goes exactly as planned for international MBA job seekers. That's why your planning must have room for a high degree of learning, evaluation, and flexibility. You must be able to respond to unexpected opportunities that come your way. Set clear goals for yourself. As you progress in your MBA experience, visualize the type of role and company you want to work for, and then work backward from there: identify what you need to do and the people you need to connect with to turn your vision into a reality. Accustomed to a predictable life that may have included both academic and professional success, many international MBA students struggle with the fact that while they may be trying extremely hard and doing all the right things, they are not nearly as in control of their destiny as they may have been in the past.

Give yourself enough freedom to attack new opportunities that arise.

Attend an info session about a firm that doesn't sponsor and that you initially may not even be interested in.

If a company coming to your university has a history of sponsorship but is in an industry you're only a little intrigued by, attend the info session. Even as a busy MBA, you should occasionally attend info sessions about companies that don't sponsor.

Get smart. Planning is great. Focus is absolutely required. But remember to carve out a bit of time for the unexpected to happen. You're in the United States, having the international adventure of your life. You just *really* never know.

Don't Ignore the Market

There's a fine line between persistence and ignoring what the market is telling you. As an international student, your time in the United States is limited after graduation if you don't have a job. If you're not getting any results, try to figure out why. Maybe staying the course is the right thing to do, maybe not. Consider such questions on a case-by-case basis, and don't make important decisions alone.

18

WHAT'S HAPPENING NEAR YOU?

An article written by Michael Dresser, which appeared in a local Maryland newspaper, had the following headline:

> *Dozens of businesses heading to India with O'Malley: Trade mission to include private deals, trade agreements*

An online publication called MarylandReporter.com ran a similar article by Len Lazarick with the headline below:

> *Back from India with deals in hand, O'Malley plans Brazil trip next year*

The former Maryland governor, Martin O'Malley, is not the only U.S. government leader who has embraced global opportunities as viable sources of growth. International students must monitor any trade activity that is happening between businesses in their college's state and their home country or region; a quick internet search will reveal any possible efforts that might be underway. Don't let these opportunities go unnoticed. Besides the possibility of networking with interesting, global individuals, these opportunities might also offer chances for you to gain some U.S. work experience by contributing a few hours a week for a small or mid-size company that's trying to establish trade relationships with your home country.

Many states even have offices abroad in order to attract investors interested in doing business with them. The Department of Business and Economic Development, through its own Maryland Center located in Shanghai, provides on-the-ground support for Maryland companies considering expansion into the China market. The office also supports Chinese companies that want to establish a business presence with the state of Maryland. I visited the Maryland Center during a trip to China in 2012 and was amazed by the resources and events that international students with an interest in doing business in Asia could leverage, even remotely.

Read on for more ways to take advantage of what's happening at the state level when planning your job search.

Small and Mid-Size Firms Need You

Google and Microsoft have the expertise and financial resources to navigate the intricacies of dealing with external markets, but small and mid-size companies may not. Yet the opportunities for these firms to sell their products and services to the world have never been greater. The web has made it all possible, but these firms don't have a vision or a process for attacking the international opportunities in front of them. This is where you come in. You have valuable market information and sophistication that can help them grow. You can show them the way. Brand yourself as an individual who can help them take their sales and profits to the next level.

Consider PetRelocation.com, a company that grows in revenues annually because more and more people expect their four-legged babies to be given the same level of care and comfort as human family members when moving to a new home. Headquartered in Austin, Texas, the company celebrated their eleventh anniversary as a business in January 2015. With a full-time staff of 35 employees, and over a hundred agents located around the globe, the staff has moved thousands of animals to every continent but Antarctica, everything from household pets to zebras and Chinese water dragons. The company's organic marketing strategy drives almost 70% of their business, via the company's website, and a significant portion of their revenue comes from global clients; more than ever, PetRelocation embraces employees with global experience to enhance their position in a niche industry. Wouldn't this be an interesting firm to launch an exciting career? The salary won't be on par with Austin-based hi-tech firms, and your friends won't recognize your employer's name, but the learning opportunities, as well as the chance to make significant contributions and leave a mark, would be tremendous for any recent college grad. Companies of all sizes are more global than ever—they have to be—and that creates all sorts of opportunities for international students, across industries and functional areas.

Intrigued by "PetRelocation" international expansion plans I decided to call them to learn more about their operations. In the course of speaking with them I probed around the types of professionals they seek to hire and they offered the statement below:

"PetRelocation happily accepts applications from F1 visa holders for post-graduation training (OPT) as well as individuals in international locations as potential agent/partners for pet shipping and export projects. People with a global perspective about business and logistics, particularly if they have benefited from living for a time outside their home country, can really relate to the key issues and concerns of our customers. That empathy and understanding can help our business grow and we are excited to work with international students in that capacity," said Kevin O'Brien, CEO and Founder of PetRelocation.com.

You know what your interests are and the impact of your skills. Your next step is to research lesser-known firms you get excited about and contact them to discuss their expansion plans. By positioning yourself as a student who wants to learn about their business, you could end up creating great job opportunities for yourself.

Virginia

According to a report called How Virginia's Economy Benefits from International Trade & Investment, published by the Virginia Economic Development Partnership, a state agency that helps develop international markets for Virginia products, 86% of Virginia exporters are small and mid-size companies with fewer than 500 workers.

It is also interesting to note that of more than 150 firms in the Richmond, Virginia, region with foreign-based parent companies, seven are subsidiaries or divisions of China-based companies, according to the Greater Richmond Partnership, a regional economic development group. Departments of business and economic development may have a focus on helping local firms expand overseas, maybe in your home country. Explore!

Smaller Firms Dominate International Business

We tend to think of global firms as large multinationals, because Google, Amazon, Microsoft, and Apple are the companies we hear about on the news every day. In terms of the number of firms involved in international business, however, smaller firms *dominate* the international business world. The International Trade Administration (ITA) works to improve the global business environment and helps U.S. organizations compete at home and abroad. In a report completed in 2011, ITA noted that "a record of more than 302,000 U.S. companies exported goods in

2011, nearly 98 percent of which (295,594) in 2011 were small or medium-sized companies (SMEs) with fewer than 500 employees."

There are 50 states in the United States, each with its own global business possibilities.

Investigate what might be happening in your state. This is a rich area of potential jobs, short-term work engagements, and networking opportunities for international MBA students.

Universities Can Help

Universities can leverage the power of their international student population by connecting them with business leaders who could greatly benefit from these students' unique knowledge and skills. Generating paid or unpaid professional opportunities for international students with smaller global firms is a viable way to help students acquire U.S. work experience while supporting the local business community's international expansion plans. As an international student, once again, always consult with your university before accepting any type of employment, paid or unpaid, to be sure you're authorized to accept it.

The USC Marshall School of Business in Los Angeles has a successful three-decade-old program where international MBA students offer consultancy services to local businesses that want to export their products in global markets. In the same metro area, the UCLA Anderson School of Management has a similar program with a slightly different focus, which also generates work opportunities for international students: executive MBA students consult with foreign companies wanting to expand into U.S. markets. At least one team member of each consultancy project is a foreign student from the country to which their client is seeking to expand.

A similar program exists at Syracuse University, where the Center for International Business helps local companies develop international business plans by employing foreign students through the Curricular Practical Training (CPT) program.

If your university has an existing program in place similar to those mentioned here, take advantage of it. But if nothing like it exists, roll up your sleeves and work with your career advisor to propose a project with specific deliverables to a firm you believe you can help. They may be thrilled to receive some consulting help from an international student who can help them gain a larger footprint in China; or they may welcome you doing a feasibility study to assess general market potential for a product they may want to export to India.

A Few Active Cities

Below are a few examples of what some cities in the United States have been doing to actively promote international trade partnerships.

Seattle has an organization called The Trade Development Alliance of Greater Seattle (TDA), whose main goal is to promote the trade interests of small and mid-size enterprises in the Seattle region in both domestic and foreign markets. For example, when a foreign delegation or related investment organization travels to the Greater Seattle region, TDA hosts an event for the delegation and invites local business leaders to attend to discuss business ideas, potential business partnerships, export strategies, and so on. These events are often open for the general public, and they would certainly provide fantastic networking opportunities for international students.

Similarly, the San Antonio Export Leaders Program, located in Texas, has a six-month program designed to increase small businesses' ability to export and expand to new markets. The program offers courses on strategy and capacity building to small-business owners. The program is a partnership with the University of Texas at San Antonio, the U.S. Department of Commerce, and the U.S. Small Business Administration. Once again, any international student looking for job leads and networking opportunities should be aware of these types of activities and explore them to the maximum.

The News from Home

Keep tabs on the news from home to find out about investment opportunities between firms from your home country and the U.S. Watch out for news about these specific areas:

- International expansion plans for mid-size U.S. companies

- Mergers

- Joint ventures

- Government approvals of relevant business projects

Ask your friends and family from home to alert you to critical business development news that might be of interest to you. If a company in your home country has purchased a U.S. corporation, you should know about it. Similarly, if a U.S. corporation acquires a firm in your home country, you should know about it as well. The newly formed organization may need people with business skills who speak the languages of both countries. This type of news might appear in a newspaper in your home country. Set up an RSS feed so you can get notified immediately of any important articles. If you're from India going to college in Maryland, for example, you might select the keywords "India," "Maryland," and "business."

Leverage your global network, particularly the contacts you have back home. Family, friends, and former employers from your home country can all provide you with job leads while you're busy studying in the United States. Someone from your home country may also be able to facilitate an informational interview for you with someone at a U.S. firm they may know. Keep your contacts at home up-to-date on your job-search efforts and ask for their assistance with your job-search goals. These are the people who have known you the longest and care the most about you. Give them a chance to help you.

Country Councils

Usually part of a chamber of commerce, country councils are valuable resources for international students looking for a job in the United States. The BRIC countries, for instance, may have dedicated councils that operate under the chamber of commerce. Resources like these must be incorporated into every international student's job-search plan. Many international students lack a basic understanding of the important economic dynamics that may be taking place between their home country and the United States. Country councils have a variety of resources you can explore to bridge this gap.

There may be networking sessions or educational seminars organized by chambers of commerce, which may be focused on your home country or region. You should attend these sessions if they are near you. If you live far away, explore their websites, give them a call, and find out ways to leverage their resources remotely. If possible, try to create a relationship with someone who works in one of these centers in case they hear about a project, job opportunity, or event you might be interested in. I once attended a session of the Brazil-U.S. Business Council in Washington, DC, and chatted with someone from Monster.com about their growth in my country, Brazil. This manager was about to open an office in Sao Paulo, Brazil and asked if I was interested in the position. I created that opportunity for myself simply because I took the initiative to join a meeting where people were talking about my country.

Explore these and other councils:

- Brazil-U.S. Business Council

- U.S.-China Business Council

- U.S.-India Business Council

International students should also find out if there are specialized consulting firms that cater to companies interested in doing business with their home country. For instance, China Channel Limited (www.chinachannelltd.com), a consulting firm in Petersburg, VA works with companies to develop markets in China. As an international student who is savvy and comfortable approaching people, you should be able to ask for an informational interview from someone who works at such a firm to try to develop a healthy list of companies you may want to target.

19

QUESTIONS FOR INTERNATIONAL MINDS TO CONSIDER

I suggest that you digest the topics in this book by engaging in discussions with your career advisor, other international students, international alumni, and anyone who has a desire to help you achieve your job-search goals. With the help of your career coach, establish goals for yourself as you implement the techniques and suggestions presented here. The value of this book is highly dependent on you executing the recommendations.

Here are a few questions to consider:

- Many of your friends from home did not go overseas for college. If you've been able to see a bit of the world, you have encountered a set of extraordinary conditions that created the opportunity for you to become an international student. What are some of the favorable conditions you grew up in, and how might they help you with your job search in the United States?

- What are some experiences that have shaped who you are culturally and globally? How can these experiences help you become a more competitive job seeker and a strong networker in general?

- How do you tell your personal story when speaking with an alumnus? How would you change this story when speaking with a recruiter? How can you reflect your depth as an international professional depending on whom you're talking to and the situation in which you find yourself?

- Do you view your international background as an asset or as baggage when job searching? Why? Be specific. Be honest with yourself.

- If you're like me, you don't believe everything you read or hear. It's a healthy habit to question the world around you, and sharp international minds should always do that. What two aspects of this book do you feel uncomfortable implementing because you're unsure about the effectiveness of the methodology or suggestion?

- Do you think you can tweak certain job-search techniques presented in this book to make them more effective for you? How?

- Forget about your job-search goals for the moment. Your life has been interesting and has shaped you in very significant ways, and now you're an international student. How can you create a story of your life that is personal, unique, and powerful, and that will make others want to learn more about you?

- In the world of college hiring, the term "international student" is used broadly. Regardless of your uniqueness as an individual and as a job seeker, this more or less becomes your label. How do you feel international students are perceived in general by U.S. recruiters and hiring managers? What are some of the positive attributes, and what are some of the negatives? How can these perceptions help you and/or hurt you as an international job seeker?

- If selling yourself is not your strength due to communication and /or cultural reasons, and knowing that employers will be assessing how confident you are when communicating your skills and accomplishments to them, how can you generate interview strategies that get you hired?

- Do you think knowing more about American football might make you more likeable or project a sense that you "fit"?

- Likability is a key hiring criteria. On a scale from 0 to 10 - 10 being extremely likeable (every wants to be around you and be your friend) how likeable are you? What number do you assign to yourself?

- How can you improve perceptions of your likeability and fit when networking and interviewing without losing yourself along the way?

- For businesses to grow, they need to experiment with new ideas, processes, and challenges every day. What level of creativity and innovation do you think you might bring to a firm because of your unique international background? Can you come up with specific examples that highlight how your unique talents will help the firms you're targeting?

- Having to collect, maintain, and build contacts in a different country is an enormously complex task for international students, who often wonder how to keep in touch after making an initial contact. What techniques from *The International Advantage* can you use to keep in touch with your newly developed contacts? How can you continue to leverage your international background in a way that is impactful, fun, honest, and *genuine* when trying to stay in touch with people?

- What defining aspects of your culture might be most interesting, powerful, and compelling to a recruiter, hiring manager, or alumnus you meet?

- Two of the most common interview questions are "Walk me through your resume" and "Tell me about yourself." Both of these present a great opportunity for you to incorporate the international aspect of your background that might tie in to the requirements of the position and/or the overall goals of the firm. Can you think of value-proposition statements that immediately differentiate you as a candidate?

- During a networking event, what personal details can you share to help lighten the mood and give people a glimpse of who you are as an international citizen? What can you tell someone you just met that suggests who you are personally, culturally, and professionally so others will want to learn more about you?

- Do you think you're an interesting person? Why? Why not?

- How can you highlight your unique and powerful traits, maybe cultural traits, when providing an interview answer using the STARE format introduced in Chapter 6, "Sharing Your Story." How can you provide an answer that directly connects with the job you're interested in?

- When international students compete with domestic students for jobs to which they don't bring something special, they tend to lose. Have you correctly identified your chances of achieving your job-search goals by assessing:

  - Accomplishments

  - Academic program

- Experience

- Personality

- Cultural strengths and traits

- Job strengths

- Passion

- Fit

- Select three jobs you're targeting and analyze the positions against the requirements listed above. What conclusions do you come to? Does your career coach agree with your conclusions? How about your mentor?

- Graduation is approaching, and you're nervous. You don't have a job. You don't have leads. You don't have a strong network. You don't want to go home. As they say in the United States: you're freaking out. How can you create meaningful forms of differentiation when targeting employers, departments, and positions that fully leverage your profile and give you a good chance of securing a U.S. job?

- Identify three roles that you feel were "created for you" and discuss these jobs with your career advisor, even if you don't feel crazy about them. Identify jobs where the fit is undeniable. Why do you feel you're such a good fit for these jobs?

- Let's say you're great at math. You did not develop this capability overnight. What do you consider to be the source of your strength, and how can you market it in a way that is highly differentiated and impactful?

- The idea of self-reliance manifests itself in a variety of ways in the United States. Can you think of a few examples of how the trait manifests itself when working with your career advisor and your career center in general?

- Employers repeatedly claim that they're looking for great problem solvers. How can you show employers that you have fresh perspectives, insights, and advanced and creative analytical and problem-solving skills that are hard to find?

- Compared to Western parents, Chinese parents spend approximately 10 times as long every day drilling their children with academic activities. By contrast, Western kids are more likely to participate in sports teams. How might these differences play out during your job search?

- If you're an MBA, generate a list of 15 companies you want to target and review the list with your career advisor. Why did you choose these companies? Do you feel your list is diversified enough? When researching the firms on your list, were you able to discover additional resources that might help you uncover new company names in the future?

- As the push to get an internship or a full-time job intensifies, many MBA students feel they don't have leads. They get stuck. That's very normal. To address this situation, how can you reach out to people you know in a genuine way, utilizing the concepts outlined on this book? How might such an outreach play out?

- An interview is a conversation. A good conversation—a good interview—is one where *both* parties are engaged. Based on what you learned in Chapters 9 and 10, what kinds of stories can you share with others that highlight your professional capabilities *and* give people a sense of who you are: your passions, your interests, and what you really care about?

- Are there lessons you can draw from situations you experienced in your country that might provide outside-the-box insights that companies need to beat their competitors? Be specific in your examples. Can you utilize your international background to see something in a way that others cannot? How?

- Can being bicultural help you develop a spot-on marketing plan for a product that needs to be launched in the United States, when U.S consumers may be weary of overused, traditional American marketing tactics? Can your lack of knowledge about the U.S. market and typical U.S. consumer behavior be an advantage you can exploit?

- Can being bicultural make you a better underwriter for mortgage securities? How?

- While European countries are accustomed to working in different languages and across borders, American business tends to be more insular. How do you achieve the right kind of balance between "fitting in" and not losing your international uniqueness when interacting with U.S. hiring managers and recruiters, who may not have had much exposure themselves to international employees?

- Can you create STARE stories that showcase the flexible thinking, risk taking, and creative problem solving that international students often have? Can you think of an instance when you thought outside the box and had the courage to bring your idea or vision to fruition?

- Are you able to list your top three strengths in less than 10 seconds? Write them down now.

- What specific steps will you take to improve your communication skills in general?

20

CONFESSIONS OF AN
INTERNATIONAL CAREER COACH

Not too long ago, as I grabbed coffee at my usual neighborhood cafe, the cashier said she'd been thinking of me because she'd heard about a *New York Times* article that discussed protests that had taken place in Brazil, sparked by controversy over whether the country should be hosting the 2014 World Cup. "I thought every Brazilian would be thrilled to be hosting the World Cup. Why the protests?" she asked me as I handed her my $2 to buy my cup of coffee.

A few months before this exchange took place, I'd heard the same cashier explain to a customer that she'd just bought some coffee from Brazil that she thought was particularly good. When it was my turn to pay for my coffee, I seized the opportunity and said, "I heard you mention that you bought some coffee from Brazil. That's where I'm from." "That's so cool," she said, with what appeared to be a genuine smile.

That was the extent of our dialogue that day, but our interactions were never the same after that. Before, I was just another customer waiting in line to buy coffee; now I'd become someone she knew something quite personal about. We'd developed a different kind of rapport. Who could better explain to this coffee shop cashier the nature of the protests that took place in my country surrounding the 2014 World Cup than me? Whenever I stood in line, this cashier acknowledged my presence in a sincere way, with a quick nod and a smile. Our interactions continued to be brief, but when the line wasn't too long, she sometimes asked me questions about my life in the United States, how it compared to life in Brazil, and why I had come to the States in the first place. Our conversations didn't involve the typical "small talk" she reserved for other customers.

When I started my job at the University of Maryland's Robert H. Smith School of Business and was first introduced to the Dean at that time, something similar happened: I mentioned that I was born in Brazil, and he said, "Brazil! I did some telecommunication research about your country years ago." Our subsequent impromptu chats in the school hallways seemed to always involve a topic related to Brazil or the world in general. I don't believe I ever got a single question from our Dean related to my job duties specifically.

I slowly learned over the years that many of my most pleasant and genuine interactions with people happened after I gave them a chance to learn something about life, my journey. I started making stronger connections with my friends, Deans of business schools, coffee-shop cashiers, managers, and neighbors. Everyone seemed genuinely eager to learn a bit more about me. I was getting asked "real" questions, and people seemed to listen to what I was saying.

It wasn't always this way. It took me years to learn that this approach was more effective for me than worrying about sounding flawless or eloquent when meeting others. When networking, as a student, I came to realize years after graduation that I was never really listening to what people were saying. What I really cared about was finding the right window of opportunity to discuss what I wanted to do professionally, hoping that those I talked to would help me advance my job search. I thought that was what I needed to do. Today, instead of bombarding people with my credentials or career history to justify my worth, I remember that the simple act of sharing where I come from seems to spark interesting and genuine conversations. It feels liberating to do this, but for a long time I didn't know it was possible. I didn't think anyone would care.

When I started my undergraduate studies at the University of Oregon at age 20, I was just another international student running around campus worried about my accent, and full of dreams, hopes, and fears. I was nervous and insecure, because I didn't understand all that was said around me. Some American students in my dorm said, "Would you like to go play intramurals?" I agreed without knowing what intramurals was, or what I was getting myself into. Watch this interview to learn more:

vimeo.com/166669059

I'm told I didn't have a thick accent when I first arrived in Oregon, but it wasn't unusual for people not to understand me from time to time. I wish I had learned sooner that remaining open and being friendly were much more important than making sure that every word coming out of my mouth was pronounced correctly. Twenty years after arriving in the United States, I still get self-conscious when I mispronounce a word though. If you think I've mastered every technique outlined in this book, you're mistaken. Some of it is still a work in progress for me.

I was so excited about the chance to study in the United States. Graduation was still some distance away, but I knew early in my college career that I was not going to be ready to go home after graduation. I wanted my international adventure to continue. However, I thought my career prospects were slim. Who would want to hire me? With zero years of full-time work experience between my undergraduate degree and my MBA—I started graduate school right after I finished my undergraduate studies—and with no major technical skills to offer employers, I thought the odds were against me. Everyone in my MBA class seemed smarter and more mature than I was, and 90% of my classmates were more experienced than I was. While the U.S. economy was strong in the late nineties, finding an employer willing to give me a work visa was not going to be easy. I was hoping that my academic credentials and sincere desire to apply myself and succeed would be enough to grab the attention of a hiring manager.

The challenges international job seekers face today are similar to the ones I once faced. The mistakes international students make when job searching remind me of my own. I don't need to ask international students what their fears or dreams are; I have had them as well. I wrote this book as one of you. I dedicate *The International Advantage* to those who are lucky enough to experience the ups and downs of being an international student looking for a job in the United States, and to those who have made this experience possible for us: in many cases, our parents. Seeing international students' potential and motivating them to achieve their career goals as global citizens is my passion, and I am now embracing it, fully, unconditionally. Thank you for embarking on this journey with me.

The Fuel for This Book

It's easy for me to empathize on a deep level with international students' job-search challenges, but the frameworks and guidelines proposed in this book are not based on my own experiences as a job seeker. My successes and struggles served as fuel to get me going with this project, but it was the time I spent working in career centers (both at the University of Maryland and at the University of Oregon) and my professional experiences in corporate America that shaped my thinking around what it takes to be successful in the U.S as a foreign national. Equally important as a source of material was the time I spent coaching and mentoring international students who trusted me to help them. Little did these students know that I was learning as much from them as they were learning from me. I also gained much insight from the numerous conversations I have had over the years with U.S. recruiters and hiring managers about international students.

I don't recall how small the world felt when I first arrived in Portland, Oregon, in 1994, but it does not seem to me that it felt as small as it is today. The explosive growth of China, India, and Brazil as true players in the world economy did not exist when I started my studies at the University of Oregon. It amazes me to receive calls from recruiters from big-name U.S. firms like IBM, HP, and Deloitte interested in targeting international students from BRIC countries. "Tell your international students that's where the action is," recruiters would tell me. And I'd respond, "I will, but how about you open your interview schedule to international students for U.S. positions next time you come to our school?"

A Hard Road for Firms, Too

It's not as easy for U.S. firms as it should be. I wonder what America's founding fathers would have had to say about the lack of progress around immigration reform. Increasing the number of H-1B visas is immediately needed. There should be no cap.

Billboards from Canada along Highway 101 linking San Francisco to Silicon Valley say: "H-1B problems? Pivot to Canada." Saudi Arabia and other countries are investing in creating national laboratory systems on par with high-quality facilities that once existed only in the United States. Guess who they want to recruit? U.S.-trained scientists, many of whom are international students. The world knows that the United States still attracts the best and the brightest—but that it also has a convoluted immigration system that can make it hard for international students to stay in the country and work after graduation.

While the United States continues to dominate when it comes to international student enrollment, the quality of higher education has improved considerably around the world. Many countries now aggressively target international students whose first option may still be to study in the United States, but who might be willing to consider cheaper high-quality options elsewhere.

More than ever this country needs to make it easy and welcoming for talented international students to apply their energy and skills in the U. S after graduation, if they choose to do so, and contribute to the growth of this great country. This is beyond economics. It's not just about doing what makes sense to help companies like Microsoft, Facebook, and Apple continue to grow. It's about injecting a dose of international diversity into U.S. society that ultimate benefits the entire world, in many different ways, at so many different levels.

Traveling the immigration path is hard—there will be more hurdles after you secure your H-1B visa—but it is certainly a worthwhile journey because the United States is an amazing country. The chance to experience life in the United States as a working professional will provide you with insights about yourself, life, and the world that you don't get as a student. Becoming a U.S. citizen was a moment of great pride for me. I welcomed my additional civic duties with open arms.

My Professional Start in the United States

I thoroughly enjoyed my years working for the firms I did, and learned a great deal about business, America, and Americans. I worked for firms that were global and hired international workers, many of whom, like me, had first arrived in the United States as international students. It was comforting to be in meetings with others who also spoke with an accent, looked a little different, and often did not understand every American football reference. Conversations among international employees about when and if our managers would file for our green cards were common. We also confided in one another and asked for help. I remember one particular instance when a group of us were discussing the meaning of the term "push back." This concept particularly frightened a Bell Labs engineer, a Ph.D. from South Korea, whose boss had told him that he expected him to push back on his ideas. This guy was truly frightened.

If Google is the default search engine today, Lucent Technologies was its equivalent in the telecommunications sector in the late nineties. I dreamed about this firm. Its size, presence in the market, and reputation: all of it impressed me. Like most MBAs, I was in love with big-name firms. I ultimately got hired into my dream job at Lucent on OPT after completing my MBA. When I met with my Lucent boss 15 years later and asked him why he'd chosen me, he answered, "Your background had made you fit to deal with change and able to learn constantly, and that's what I was looking for in my new hire." My first manager wasn't talking about my MBA or even the specific skills that had made me competitive for the role. He was using the word "background" on a much higher level. Did he understand the value of where I came from? How could he know that the circumstances I'd grown up in had made me adaptable and resilient, able to deal with the personal and professional changes he had the foresight to anticipate? For a minute, I thought he did know. I flourished at Lucent, despite the radical changes impacting the telecom sector around 2002.

Still Working to Develop U.S Assertive Communication Style

At a popular breakfast stop in my neighborhood one morning, I observed a conversation between a mother and her son that caught my attention. The mother asked her boy - her son could not have been more than about 4 years old - if he wanted a whole-wheat bagel for breakfast, and the boy responded, "No, Mom, I don't want that. I want the chocolate-chip bagel, please." I was in awe. This little boy was so comfortable telling his mother what his preferences were. Not just that: his mother listened to him and honored his wish. In the end, he got what he wanted at age 4. When he grows up, he'll have no problem letting the world know what he wants out of life. He will have no problem negotiating a raise for himself.

For a few seconds, I was a little jealous of that boy. He effortlessly communicated with a level of confidence I am not able to at times. But then I hadn't been given the same opportunities. When I was a child, my mom never asked me what I wanted to eat. While my dad was working, she made decisions on my behalf: what I should have for breakfast, who my friends should be, what I should study in college, how I should go about managing life in general.

Recognizing that I might not be able to catch up to that little boy's assertive communication style doesn't mean I don't try, but it does mean I can be more patient with myself. Over the years, I have gotten much better at laughing at myself and being vulnerable. I've realized that if I embrace who I am, with all my country-specific skills and traits, and apply all of it courageously in a new context, I can be enormously successful and fulfilled. That's the focus! I live in a different world now. I'm predisposed to behave in certain ways because of where I'm from. I embrace the good and bad that comes along with that. Finding my sweet spot has become much more important than expecting myself to "perform" at unrealistic levels. International students are sitting on a gold mine of talents. I hope your international adventure will bring you closer to understanding what those are for you.

This Book

The more individuals who undertake research in the field of career development for international students the better off we'll all be. I hope this book has an immediate impact on the lives of international students who seek to remain in the United States as working professionals after graduation. Furthermore, if this book creates intelligent dialogue among the various groups of individuals who interact with international students, such as academics, policy makers, career advisors, HR managers, and hiring managers of large and small firms, then it will have achieved all that it stands for.

The International Advantage was never meant to be an exhaustive job search guide. This is not the only book international students will need to read to achieve their job-search goals. You may have noticed that I didn't cover a few important topics, such as social media. LinkedIn has emerged as the #1 tool every job seeker must use, but I don't address it in depth here. My reason is that I know career centers across the country offer excellent help with social media, as well as other areas that aren't addressed in this book. That said, I hope your social-media strategy incorporates the key concepts that are covered here in detail. When you get ready to ask someone via LinkedIn for an informational interview, or even to connect with you, the frameworks we discussed should give you confidence. Once you meet with a professional you want to learn from, remember that revealing who you are will immediately set the stage for a great conversation.

An Apology

The stories I have featured in this book, while 100% real—only the names of the international students were changed—are not representative of the diversity of career interests international students have. I wish I had a much bigger sample of non-MBA international students' job-search stories to choose from, and I hope you can help me fix this issue in the next edition of this book. I'm committed to collecting more MBA stories because they're always full of drama and excitement, but I'm also determined to find different types of stories from international students from different majors next time.

A Request for International Students

Any suggestions you may have for how to make this book more valuable for international students are welcomed and needed. Please email me at marcelobarrosmba@gmail.com. I do hope to hear from you. Similarly, it would be wonderful if you shared your experiences as an international job seeker so others can learn from you. Maybe it is now time for you to tell the world your story, with an open heart. Are you ready? I hope so.

I created a website www.theinternationaladvantage.com which has a tab called "Share Your Story", which is waiting for your words. Write as much or as little as you would like. Whatever you have to say or share might help an international student out there run the job search marathon with more confidence.

Seek Out the "A-ha!" Moments

When surrounded by culturally familiar people, I can often anticipate how people may react to my suggestions. Sometimes I know what they'll say before they say it. "A-ha!" moments are rare. But when individuals with different points of view, work styles, and cultures get together to attack a problem, then the team has an opportunity to reach a level of creativity and spontaneity often not available for teams comprised of individuals who all grew up in the same country. Some U.S. employers sponsor international students only when finding a qualified U.S. citizen to fill a role is difficult. Becoming a progressive global enterprise means letting go of this narrow view. Companies that hire people who have all read the same books, are products of the same educational system, grew up in the same country, speak the same language, and watch the same TV channels are missing the boat. Progressive firms should intentionally inject different accents into their pool of employees.

Don't let the magic of being international go away. Hold on to it. Use it to shine in interviews. Use it when you start working right after graduation, throughout your stay in the United States, or wherever else life takes you. Change the conversation. Always remain fresh, interesting, and global. Be vigilant about "fitting in" too much. Remember the wonderful message that Yang Zhao shared with us all. Show others how differentiated your thinking is. Hiring managers—smart ones, at least—are looking for that. Don't be just another candidate: you can do better. When you get the job you want, be the kind of professional that will generate breakthroughs in whatever it is you choose to do. You have the potential to do so. It would be a shame if you didn't. Show others your alert and questioning mind, and your ability to see interesting combinations, possibilities, and solutions.

It's an honor to be part of the closed world that international students sometimes live in. Moving forward, I know you'll apply maximum focus and energy on fully exploiting the extraordinary opportunities available to you.

What you've accomplished in life already is awesome. Savor your days as an international student. Create exciting and interesting experiences for yourself so when you look back at your international adventure—no matter where life takes you—you'll have wonderful memories and a connection with the world which will serve you well in various aspects of your life. You've been blessed with the opportunity of a lifetime, the opportunity to be an international student. This world belongs to us. Best of luck out there. I'm rooting for you.

21

ADDITIONAL READING FOR CAREER SERVICES PROFESSIONALS

In addition to the resources footnoted and mentioned throughout this book, what follows are selected materials that directly or indirectly helped me write *The International Advantage*, and which I recommend as additional reading to career services professionals who work with international students.

Those who work closely with international students might find the research conducted by Leong and Sedlack (1987) a good starting point for understanding the practical and impractical career development needs of international students. The authors published a paper called "Academic and Career Needs of International and United States College Students," which includes survey results indicating that the majority of international students feel a greater need for counseling and career education compared to American students. The authors state that "services tailored to their needs will have to be developed if they are to be effective."

In a paper written by Frederick T. L. Leong, Erin E. Hardin, and Arpana Gupta called "A Cultural Formulation Approach to Career Assessment and Career Counselling with Asian Americans" (*Journal of Career Development* 37(1), 465-486, Curators of the University of Missouri 2010), the authors allude to an integrated model of cross-cultural counselling proposed by Leong, which suggests that an individual exists on three levels: the universal, the group, and the individual. If the role of a career advisor is to help students become more self-aware and uncover jobs and careers that fit them, then culture as a variable needs to be an integral part of the career-counselling process. In their study, the authors offer the following insight: "For a career theorist to ignore cultural factors by restricting career development solely to attaining personal interests and implementing personal values is not only inaccurate but potentially dangerous for those individuals who come from a collectivistic cultural framework."

Along the same lines but with a much more contemporary twist, the short discussion in Chapter 4, "The Impact of Culture," has been inspired by Malcolm Gladwell's book *Outliers* (Little, Brown, 2008). The concept of cultural strengths is what I particularly wanted to draw attention to. When one is operating outside of his or her element, these factors take on important new dimensions and make us think about "fit" in different ways.

Finally, career services professionals who like to monitor the world of H-1B visas on a very macro level may want to get to know The Brookings Institution (www.brookings.edu). This organization conducts research on immigration and regularly publishes reports that help us all understand, for instance, how H-1B visas are being used, and by whom.

Acknowledgments

Desperate to help myself, I started going to my college career center to find support. I must have spent so much time at the University of Oregon (UO) Career Center that they figured they might as well hire me. For four years I immersed myself in the world of jobs, careers, recruiters, resumes, work visas, and career counselors and the confusion all of these can bring to international students. On a personal level, my years at the UO Career Center allowed me to receive great help regarding which graduate programs to apply to and what career paths to consider.

The wonderfully talented staff I worked with, led by Dr. Larry Smith, sensed my desire to help myself and other international students with career-related matters. Together we partnered with other departments and created some infrastructure to better address the job-search needs of the international-student community. We worked on brochures called "Job Search Strategies for International Students" and organized workshops called "Global Careers" for students who were globally minded. To this day, I am still proud of what we accomplished. We weren't just talking with international students about visas. We understood that there was much more we could and needed to do. Recently I realized that the blueprint for *The International Advantage* was created during the years I spent running around the UO Career Center.

Perhaps no greater testament to being great at what you do is having those who watch you feel so inspired that they want to follow in your footsteps. You project peace in your actions and decisions. Others are affected by your calm energy and want to be part of what you're doing. You are this consummate professional, Dr. Magid Shirzadegan. No matter what, you always told us it would be okay. I miss being a Peer Assistant. I knew I was going to circle back to our world. You're responsible for me coming home. Here I am.

I also need to express my gratitude to Wayne and Rita Kingsbury, the first people I met in the United States when I entered this country as an international student. You never let us feel alone. You have given us all much emotional and material support. Your hearts and your home were always open for us. We shared our achievements and successes with you, and you were close to us when things did not go well. You help me keep my great memories from beautiful Oregon alive.

I also wanted to acknowledge the help I received from the International MBAs below. In typical MBA fashion, these students spoke their minds, and their contributions ranged from edits to structural suggestions to "Get rid of all this material, Marcelo. It doesn't offer any value."

My special thanks go to:

Anant Bhatia, MBA, from India

Miao Zhao, MBA, from China

And then there is Shruti Suresh, MBA from India, who agreed to be part of this project and graciously let me profit from her extensive background in editing and content writing. I am so glad you came into my life, Shruti, to help me get across the finish line. And thank you Margo Orlando Littell, my editor, who was with me from the beginning.

Thank you Steve Passiouras from bookow.com for being fast, efficient, and for formatting The International Advantage beautifully. You are a life saver.

The assistance I received from the career services professionals mentioned above, as well as the encouragement I received from the aforementioned international students, mattered most. It's funny how, in the end, it often comes down to us finding people who believe in us.

Thank you Rafael Cravo da Silva Barros for your contributions regarding how to market *The International Advantage.* I love your "Night of Autographs" idea Rafa. Let's do some of these together.

Fernanda Cravo da Silva Barros drawing skills and artistic intuition helped me finalize the book cover. Thank you Fefe.

While I am sincerely grateful for the wonderful assistance I received from each of the individuals I just recognized, I am the one directly responsible for the final content of this book.

And last but not least, my biggest and most important thank-you goes to my parents. Mom and Dad: like both of you, I remain dumbfounded as to how I got infected by the international virus. It is a wonderful bug to have, I must say. It doesn't seem like it was transmitted to me by either of you, although you, Dad, sometimes seem to exhibit symptoms of someone who could also have the virus. Maybe it's been dormant? We should wake it up and see a bit of the world together again. Willi Barros and Marlene Barros: um grande beijo pra voces dois. Muito obrigado por tudo. Your love allows me to reach for higher ground, and in many ways I am able to embrace my fears and vision because of you. Mom: though you never asked me what I wanted to have for breakfast, I forgive you, because you're still my best career coach, and I'll need your guidance moving forward. I know you won't be shy about telling me exactly what I need to do.

.

Made in the USA
Columbia, SC
08 November 2023

25724908R00159